GOD @ WORK

VOLUME 2

DEVELOPING MINISTERS IN THE MARKETPLACE

GOD @ WORK

VOLUME 2

DEVELOPING MINISTERS IN THE MARKETPLACE

RICH MARSHALL

with Ken Walker

Destiny Image® Publishers, Inc.
P.O. Box 310
Shippensburg, PA 17257-0310

"Speaking to the Purposes of God for This Generation
and for the Generations to Come"

ISBN 0-7684-2266-3

For Worldwide Distribution
Printed in the U.S.A.

This book and all other Destiny Image, Revival Press, MercyPlace, Fresh Bread, Destiny Image Fiction, and Treasure House books are available at Christian bookstores and distributors worldwide.

4 5 6 7 8 9 10 / 09 08 07

To place a book order, call toll-free: **1-800-722-6774**.
For more information on foreign distributors, call **717-532-3040**.
Or reach us on the Internet:

www.destinyimage.com

Acknowledgments

To my wife, Wilma, who never ceases to pray for me.

To Ken Walker whose skills greatly enhance mine.

*To the ROi team who believes in me
and in this important message.*

Contents

CHAPTER 1

From Principles to Practice

So let us stop going over the basics of Christianity again and again. Let us go on instead and become mature in our understanding (Hebrews 6:1 NLT).

When we flew to the Caribbean island of Barbados on a balmy September afternoon, my wife, Wilma, and I were en route to a Labor Day weekend of rest and relaxation with our friends, Kyffin and Roberta Simpson. Our trip included one work-related task: a Saturday morning seminar I would conduct for local business leaders.

On Friday afternoon Kyffin, his son, David, and I were body surfing just off a picturesque beach. None of us were too concerned about the approach of Hurricane Ivan, although we chatted a little about it. The hurricane would soon become the third of four to wallop the Caribbean and U.S. mainland over a six-week period. But this day, news about Ivan maintained a low profile in Barbados, especially since the island sits outside the annual hurricane season's customary path.

However, by the next morning at the seminar, a number of audience members were discussing the possibility of Ivan striking

Barbados three days later. Seeing the number of worried looks slowly spreading, I decided to use this situation as a real-life example of what I would discuss during the general session.

After opening with an explanation of God's call to work and the authority we have in the name of Jesus, I told the group, "Let's stand up and exercise our authority over this storm. Let's pray these three things: 1) that the wind slows down; 2) that the storm turns before it arrives in Barbados; and 3) that there is no damaging rain accompanying the hurricane."

Everyone stood. As I directed them, they put their hands toward the east and prayed this prayer of faith with me. I thought nothing of this; I've led prayers of this nature many times over the past four decades. As of 1999 and after 35 years as a pastor, I have made my living speaking, writing, and teaching about God's activity in the marketplace.

Usually, when I speak at conferences Christians tend to make up 90 percent of the crowd. But this day, I learned that more than 80 percent did not claim to follow Christ, nor were most used to praying this way, even those who expressed a Christian faith. Still, they all cooperated. Afterward, I went on with my presentation.

When the seminar concluded, we continued tracking Ivan's progress on the Internet for the rest of Saturday, Sunday, and Monday. As some feared, Barbados lay right in the center of the storm's path. On Labor Day the trade publication, *Insurance Journal*, carried a Web report headlined "Caribbean Islands Brace for Another Hurricane; Ivan Now a Category 4 Storm."

About 20 miles across and 40 miles long, Barbados is only about two and a half times the size of Washington, D.C. Considering that the hurricane itself measured several times the size of the island, there appeared to be little chance Ivan would spare us his fury. Given the ominous signs, on Monday night, Wilma and I stood with the Simpson family on the cliff's edge of their property. We prayed the same prayer we had on Saturday morning and then went to bed.

By that time, the hurricane had moved within 100 miles of this island nation. In the morning, the time forecasters projected Ivan would reach full strength, we awoke to the relative calm of winds in the 40 to 50 mile-per-hour range. Stiff, to be sure, but far below a hurricane's minimum force. Granted, there were problems, such as widespread power outages, downed utility poles and trees, and lost roofs. I saw a picture of one woman whose small home had to be torn down because of damage.

Still, compared to what had been forecast, we saw a dramatic answer to prayer. The winds had slowed, the hurricane had turned, and the rain did not come. I realize that Ivan devastated other Caribbean nations, particularly nearby Grenada. While I have no explanation for that, I believe that I understand what the Lord did in Barbados.

First of all, we had just met with a group of people who needed a booster shot for their faith. As a sign of His power, God loves to perform miracles for those who do not yet know Him. For example, I once talked with evangelist Carlos Anacondia of Argentina about some of the miracles that regularly occurred during his popular crusades in the 1990s. There were times when people with cavities had their teeth miraculously filled during his meetings. Yet, Anacondia's children still had to go to the dentist.

In addition (and this is of paramount significance), we had gathered with a group of leaders who had been convened by one of Barbados' most prominent business leaders. Kyffin Simpson's reputation is as well known as his business successes. A man of great influence throughout the Caribbean, he is known as a person whose faith in God comes first in his life.

I believe God is placing His leaders in positions of influence for the sake of His Kingdom (which hereafter I will capitalize). The week following that event in Barbados, residents were buzzing about how God had turned the hurricane aside. This can happen when a business leader has as much Christian influence as financial and business success.

I believe the Simpsons' faithful God-centered business leadership set the stage for the Lord's intervention. Wilma and I were simply there as messengers at the right time.

Influencing Nations

Do you want to develop skills as a Marketplace Minister? Do you want to influence your city and your nation for the Lord? If so, this book is for you. Several years ago I wrote *God@Work* for the purpose of releasing and encouraging Christians to fulfill their destiny and purpose in the workplace. This follow-up volume is intended to help you function in this growing field of ministry, presenting ideas that will help you put these principles into practice.

God@Work: Volume 2 includes the stories of a number of business figures, all of whom I know personally. All have been impacted in some fashion by the marketplace ministry message and are making a difference in their spheres of influence. In turn, all these people have had an impact on me by faithfully fulfilling God's call on their lives.

Kyffin Simpson is one of these men. He read *God@Work* because of his son's encouragement. He then attended a conference where I spoke; another of his sons had organized that seminar. Kyffin is now a dear friend. I know that God is giving him tremendous favor in his nation and throughout the Caribbean.

To give you an idea of how he is viewed at home, consider the speech complimenting him when the University of the West Indies recently awarded him an honorary doctor of laws degree:

> Chancellor, Kyffin Donald Simpson has reached the summit of a stellar business career. Tonight, in receiving an honorary doctorate of our beloved university, he achieves the summit of his academic career. And as he was most appropriately born at a house called The Summit, in the parish of St John, he has truly come full circle!
>
> Kyffin was educated at the Lodge School, a few hundred yards from his home, and then in the UK. Earlier this

week he returned from halfway across the globe—Japan—a trip he makes as often as those he once made, that short distance, like Shakespeare's schoolboy, "with his satchel and shining morning face, creeping like a snail, unwillingly, to school!"

Soon after founding the Simpson Group of companies 30 years ago, he went to Japan to seek out the franchise for Suzuki, in response to the horrendous impact of the energy crisis on the Caribbean. He made Suzuki the number-one selling car in Barbados and among the top three in the Caribbean for 20 years. He helped to establish a major presence for the brand in the Caribbean, including Puerto Rico, and in Brazil, as well as assisting its entry into Europe and the USA.

He's also responsible for bringing Skoda and Porsche into Barbados, and bringing back Mercedes-Benz and Chrysler. The range of Simpson Motors covers both basic needs and the dreams on wheels, of every car obsessed man, and quite a few women!

Kyffin Simpson is acknowledged as one of the most innovative executives in the automobile industry in the Caribbean and Latin America.

He is widely regarded as the leading international entrepreneur in Barbados and a role model in the private sector for companies wanting to demonstrate international competitiveness by penetrating global markets. And he has a reputation for investing in the development of his own company's workers. But his international reach includes membership of the Board of the prestigious Americas Society and Council of the Americas.

His strong faith in God, whose blessings he acknowledges in every aspect of his life, fuels his passion to sow something back into the work of those who promote the word of God.

But his benevolence also includes local sport and popular culture. His sponsorships enabled the phenomenal career advancement of two young Bajan sporting icons—Ronald "Suki" King and Barry Forde. King's career, from Bridgetown working-class community to world draughts champion, has inspired many "boys on the block," and revived a game long considered marginal. And Barry's emergence as world champion cyclist demonstrated commitment and reward for that trust.

Kyffin Simpson is the epitome of service. He enjoys the blessing of loving his work; of working with things he loves—cars—and serving the God of love. And in the Queen's New Year's Honours list of 2004 he was awarded the Commander of the British Empire (CBE) for his contribution to business in the Caribbean.

Chancellor, we have much to learn from this very model of a Caribbean businessman; and I invite you to admit him to that inner circle, by conferring on this great friend and benefactor the degree of Doctor of Laws, honoris causa.[1]

Notice where this man is making an impact:

- In the business arena, where he is known as "the leading international entrepreneur in Barbados."

- In government, where "his international reach includes membership on the Board of the prestigious Americas Society and Council of the Americas."

- In the sporting culture, where his sponsorships further the career advancement of two young Bajan sports stars.

- I was especially impressed with the sentence: "His strong faith in God, whose blessings he acknowledges in every aspect of his life, fuels his passion to sow something back into the work of those who promote the word of God."

This man is an example of a Marketplace Minister. (From here on, I will use the term Marketplace Minister in its capitalized form to speak of those in the marketplace who recognize that they are called to this ministry.) Simpson has been called to serve in the business arena, and as he answers God's summons, his influence is spreading. Consider the following news story:

> As a result of the purchase of Shell Antilles and Guianas Limited's petroleum distribution and marketing businesses throughout the Caribbean, the Sol Group will form the first major regional oil business based in the Caribbean, one that combines international reach with local expertise.
>
> Sol is the petroleum affiliate of Interamericana Trading Corp (ITC), an international conglomerate with automotive, telecommunications and banking interests in over 32 countries across Latin America, Central America, the Caribbean, the U.S. and Europe. Founded in 1974 by its chairman, Kyffin Simpson, ITC employs over 1,700 staff across the world from its Caribbean headquarters and distributes and markets more than 40,000 cars each year from Porsche, Daimler-Chrysler, General Motors, Skoda and Suzuki through a global dealer network and commercial accounts.
>
> It is the Caribbean's leading automotive group and has played a key role in turning Suzuki into the number one selling brand in the region. ITC and Sol have the resources and expertise required to invest for growth in the regional oil sector.
>
> The Sol Group will acquire Shell's petroleum distribution and marketing businesses in Barbados, St. Lucia, Netherlands Antilles, Dominica, Antigua, St. Kitts & Nevis, British

Virgin Islands, Anguilla, Grenada, St. Vincent, Guyana, Suriname and Belize. This transaction will include the purchase of Shell Antilles & Guianas Ltd, Shell Belize Ltd. and the Shell Suriname Verkoopmaatschappij N.V.

As part of this, Sol will take over existing staff, commercial contracts and associated obligations. Sol will continue to use the Shell brand under license at its service stations, and act as the sole distributor of Shell's fuels and lubricants in the countries which form part of the acquisition.

The Sol Group represents a new approach to the oil industry as the first major regional oil business based in the Caribbean.

According to chairman of the Sol Group, Kyffin Simpson, in a media release on the company, the Sol Group will be a regional organisation run from local offices and will invest to grow the business as a central part of the acquisition. Sol has recruited top executive management from the oil industry with decades of experience at senior levels and widespread international exposure and expertise.

Sol will be a leading employer offering rewarding, long term careers for its people with a focus on the development of local talent and expertise. A customer-centered organisation and an emphasis on growth and excellence means significantly more responsibility for staff, more focus on individuals and, ultimately, the potential to share in the financial benefits of success, noted Simpson.

This same approach will allow Sol to be highly responsive to the needs of customers. Significant investment in new systems, technology and business opportunities will underline an innovative approach to growth for business and the region. This will all be backed by Sol's position as exclusive supplier of Shell's world class fuels and lubricants.

As a regional company, Sol will invest in the Caribbean… collaborating closely with local governments and customers. It will also offer significant additional employment and training opportunities for…nationals, combined with an understanding of the needs of both customers and the territories in which it operates. Sol will manage its operations and adopt Health, Safety and Environmental standards in line with international industry practice, Simpson pointed out.[2]

Entering the Marketplace

The week after Hurricane Ivan passed through the Caribbean, Wilma and I were talking with Kyffin and Roberta about how we could reach whole nations for Christ. For years this had been our desire. It represented the motivating influence in my decision to leave a local church to start a ministry to marketplace leaders. As our conversation continued, I could see how God had guided me to this very place.

To set the stage for what was occurring, I had known without a doubt that God had called me to do what I was doing: leading conferences and seminars on how businesspersons could bring God's influence into the marketplace. After leaving the relative security of the pastorate, I had spent six financially challenging years speaking to Christian businesspeople about the call of God in their lives, in the place where they spend most of their time—the office.

Since 1999, this journey had taken me to more than 100 cities across the U.S. and 25 nations. I felt like the Lord had taught me valuable lessons about His plan to impact cities and nations through business. Little did I know that He would then tell me to quit talking about it and start doing it. A few months before heading to Barbados I sensed the Lord saying, "Rich, I want you to start a business."

Although that stunned me, this was one of the clearest messages I had ever heard. That directive continued to run through my mind and I sought the Lord for the specifics of how this would work. Now I could see this meeting as one more step in the process that God was leading me through to impact cities and nations for His Kingdom.

Starting a business was not on our minds when we embarked on this journey, but looking back, we can see the hand of the Lord each step of the way. By the time we landed in Barbados we felt the Lord had revealed His direction. Since my gift is in speaking, and my background is as a pastor, a business that could incorporate those two characteristics would be ideal.

I found this in the corporate training field, where I could speak to business leaders on the practical aspects of business—namely, the people side as opposed to the technical aspects. In such a business, I could speak to the ethics (or lack of) operating in the corporate culture. I could organize a firm to address such relevant topics as problem solving, conflict resolution, leadership skills, communication skills, and behavior styles. We would also focus on building purpose in business with sessions on character, ethics, and principles.

This was all in the final planning stages when we traveled to Barbados, but we had not yet launched the business. So on the day that Wilma and I talked with the Simpsons about reaching nations, I mentioned this as a strategy.

"Why not impact nations by changing the businesses one by one?" I asked. "If we can bring principles and character and ethics back to corporations, we can change the nations from the inside out. We have been trying to impose change from the outside through preaching. Let's bring about change from the inside and see what God will do."

"That's what I believe too," Roberta Simpson responded. "Let's start with our company here in Barbados."

Later I met with Debbie Simpson, the general manager. She agreed that we should do leadership training with the corporation's top level managers. This company is the ideal place to start. It has strong Christian leadership, a foundation of ethics and principles, and a supportive owner. However, not all its employees are Christians. Not all of them fully understand, or agree with, the Judeo Christian principles that guide management decisions.

We put together a dozen half-day sessions to build the leadership skills of the management team. Because of scheduling challenges within the company, and travel, we scheduled six consecutive days of training for 25 managers and then another six days with 25 other managers. This rapid launch of our business went well; we received enthusiastic evaluations. Even skeptics proved receptive, responding with such comments as:

> "Thank you for reinforcing what I knew in my heart to be right and showing me how to apply this knowledge to my work."

> "This was the only training workshop that encouraged me to want to make a difference in the way I do my job."

> "For the first time in fifty years, I now understand myself through your course, which will enable me to understand coworkers and more important will improve my personal life 100 percent."

I share this personal story to make several points.

1. God wants us to use every means possible to impact cities and nations for His Kingdom. Over the past 40 years, Wilma and I have done a thorough job of church planting, church growth seminars, and evangelism. Especially in developed nations, the Christian message is strongly promoted. Yet, many unreached people groups exist in developing nations. I am concerned about them, too. We have not impacted every level of society through traditional church expansion. This is where business ministry enters the picture; God is presently calling forth leaders in every sphere of influence.

2. I do not believe that every Christian should start a business, any more than I believe that every pastor should start a new church. However, I do believe that all of us need to find the place where our

impact is the greatest. Then, prepare ourselves for the coming move of God that will involve the transformation of cities and nations. I was surprised when the Lord told me to start a new business, but I knew that this was His plan.

3. You are never too old to embrace goals and new dreams. As you age, you may not be able to run as fast or as far, but you can run to the fulfillment of your dreams. In *Passages*, author Gail Sheehy writes about three adulthoods. The third begins around age 60, when you discover who you are and begin to take back your life. This is the time for which God has prepared you. Sadly, many of God's greatest leaders are thinking of retirement in the very season the Lord has prepared them for their greatest years of effective service.

I often tell Bishop Bill Hamon of Christian International Ministries Network—based in Santa Rosa Beach, Florida—that I want to be like him when I grow up. He is ten years older, has been married ten years longer, has been serving the Lord ten years longer, and has been a Marketplace Ministry leader ten years longer. He and his wife, Evelyn, recently celebrated 50 years of ministry service. The celebration didn't mark his retirement; it simply launched him into his next phase of service.

Often when I speak, there are a number of retirees in the audience. Usually one of them will say something like this: "I wish I had heard this message 30 years ago when I could have used it." My response: "You can still be used by the Lord today. Find that place where your gifts, skills, talents, and experience can be used. Sometimes it may be as an advisor, sometimes as a leader, and sometimes as an intercessor, but for sure there is a place for you."

4. Get yourself ready because you may not know ahead of time the moment that the Lord will propel you toward the fulfillment of your dream. It is time to make preparations. Go back to school, read more books, develop your skills, and get ready. At age 70, Louisiana governor Mike Foster enrolled in law school. Colonel Harlan Sanders was in his 60s when Kentucky Fried Chicken—now

KFC—finally rose to prominence. John Glenn rode aboard the space shuttle, Discovery, at the age of 77.

What are you doing to get ready for the next phase of impact in your life? I am starting a multinational company for leadership development. In addition to training business leaders, I will be consulting with affiliates scheduled to open in ten nations over the next three years. This isn't because I am amazing, but because God has led me to this stage in my life and made it possible.

What new vistas await you? I am confident that as you read, the Lord will lead you toward a more satisfying and rewarding future for you and your family. If you doubt this possibility, turn to the next chapter to read about a business innovator in England who is bringing change to a suburb of London.

Endnotes

1. Henry Fraser, *Barbados Daily Nation* (online), Nov. 28, 2004. Available from www.nationnews.comStoryView.cfm?Record=55624.

2. "Sol to form regional-based oil business," *The Barbados Advocate* (online), Nov. 8, 2004. Available from www.barbadosadvocate.com/NewViewNewsleft.cfm?Record=19248.

CHAPTER 2

The Coming Army

For the Son of Man has come to seek and to save that which was lost (Luke 19:10).

Imagine a city where 1,000 new ministers have been identified, equipped, and released into multiple spheres of influence. Some serve in government, while others work in retail shops or as school-teachers. They are business leaders who see their marketplace as an opportunity to touch people's lives and lift them out of the hum-drum of daily survival. This movement includes figures from the worlds of entertainment and media. Meanwhile, local congregations are working together to identify and train these Marketplace Ministers.

Sound like a dream? Think this only happened in the Book of Acts? This is reality today in Guildford, England, one of the many suburbs surrounding London, the world's second largest city. What may be most amazing of all is that it took a businessman to plant the vision of this renewal and then transform it into daily life.

Julian Watts is a business leader in this bustling city. In 2002, Watts was experiencing his own period of spiritual growth when he felt compelled to ask a group of pastors if he could join their interdenominational prayer group. After they welcomed him, this soft-spoken company president, who gained considerable business experience with a multinational consulting firm, assembled plans that would impact the entire city.

Today, the activity in Guildford is likely to become a benchmark for other cities across the world. Julian has now spoken in most of Guildford's churches. Because of his leadership and encouragement, surveys have been circulated that have helped identify more than 1,000 Christians who affirm that their primary ministry exists in the workplace.

Why Guildford? I mention Julian because he is the obvious point man. However, behind the scenes, hidden away in a boardroom in a technical center, about 30 business leaders have been meeting regularly for the past four years. They were called together by Richard Fleming, a London-based business consultant.

My wife, Wilma, and I met Richard and Pauline Fleming several years ago, and have been fascinated to watch them mentor businesspeople in the art of hearing the voice of God. Richard and Pauline, along with a group of fellow marketplace ministers, have been seeking to hear the voice of God for their city, formulate divinely directed strategies, and discern the Lord's agenda for Guildford.

Under the Flemings' direction, they have formed what is known as a Kingdom Advice Centre (to use the British spelling). A practical training tool for workplace leaders, it focuses on how to hear the voice of God in a business setting. Since most training has come in church environments, to date, much of the "hearing" has been interpreted in church language. For example, one might hear a call to minister and assume that it means to pastor a church. At a Kingdom Advice Centre, it is interpreted in the context of the workplace. (You can read more about this in Chapter 8, "Hearing the Voice of God.")

Although they all are ministers, none of these participants bears the traditional identity of a pastor wearing a clerical collar. Yet they are marketplace ministers, led by a Marketplace Minister named Richard. As they hammered the heavens with their prayers, God responded through another Marketplace Minister named Julian.

Even though these two marketplace leaders had not seen each other for a long time, years ago they had worked together. With Julian as the owner of a company, and Richard as his managing director, the Lord taught them to trust in Him, hear His voice, and follow His leading. Years later, God brought them together again as an answer to those earlier prayers. God used Julian as a catalyst for the city. Now Richard is using his experience to help train and release the 1,000 newly identified ministers for Guildford. As business leaders use work as a ministry platform, it is drawing an entire city toward potential transformation.

Redeeming Work

The story of Guildford emphasizes this truth: Work is not a curse. For far too many years in Christian circles, work has gotten a "bad rap." This impression has developed because of a regrettable fact. Although we have told the truth about how the redemption Jesus offers affects the world, we have not told the *whole truth*. Although not malicious in our intent, this tendency has caused considerable confusion among masses of Christians.

A prime example is the story of Jesus' encounter with Zacchaeus, which appears in Luke 19:1-10. This is the passage where Zacchaeus, a chief tax collector, climbs a tree to catch a glimpse of Christ. After Jesus comes to his home, Zacchaeus is overcome with emotion and pledges, "Behold, Lord, the half of my goods I will give to the poor; and if I have taken anything from any man by false accusation, I restore him fourfold" (v. 8 KJV). At the conclusion of this story, Jesus says, "For the Son of Man has come to seek and to save that which was lost" (v. 10).

It may sound like hairsplitting, but notice the use of "that." Jesus did not say that He came to seek and save "those" who were lost. Now, surely He did come to save lost people. It is appropriate for us to proclaim this truth to everyone we can, with the intent of bringing them into the Kingdom of God. However we have usually stopped there.

At the risk of sounding overly simplistic, I would point out "that" includes "those," but "those" does not include "that." When Jesus said that He came to seek and to save "that" which was lost, it represented an inclusive statement. Certainly He spoke of the souls of men and women. However, His statement also refers to *everything else that was lost* when sin entered the world. When we teach people about the power of the blood of Jesus to bring redemption, we need to include the reality that He also redeemed our work life.

The second chapter of Genesis introduces work as God planned it: a wondrous, inspiring combination of God's work and human cooperation. God did not plan for labor to be backbreaking, sweat-inducing, anxious toil. Instead, He designed it so humans could help Him care for the earth. Meditate on that for a moment. Almighty God, for whom nothing is impossible, created the world with a plan for men and women to help tend His creation. Awareness of this reality will revolutionize your attitude toward your Monday-through-Friday routine.

Work is not a result of the curse that came when humans sinned. However, the tension-filled, heart attack-producing, high blood pressure-inducing stress often present in offices, on assembly lines, and in countless other workplaces originated with Adam and Eve's disobedience. The good news is Jesus died to release us from this curse. When Christ spoke the words recorded in Luke 19:10, He assured mankind that He would take care of everything stained by humans' wrongdoing.

When we introduce people to Jesus and convince them to place their trust in Him, we should tell them about more than Christ's ability to forgive their willful mistakes. We need to tell them about His power to introduce a stress-free approach to work into their lives. We need to remind them of the Garden of Eden's peaceful environment, which illustrates God's desire to bless the work of their hands.

Work is a part of God's plan for everyone's life, but not as typically presented. We need to start telling the whole truth regarding God's plan. If we fail, we leave people in bondage. That is sad, because the Lord paid the price to remove those chains and set people free to live the way He intended.

As I travel across the world, I proclaim this message: God wants to bless you in your work! He cares about what you do. His desire is that you prosper in all ways. Too often this is interpreted only in materialistic terms. However, God also wants to bless your marriage, family, friendships, and work relationships while giving you a sense of deep personal fulfillment in your vocation. Apply the sacrifice Jesus made for mankind, and you can find redemption and restoration in every way.

Gambling for Wealth

Ever been in a church service? Usually, just before the sermon comes an offering. The pastor relies on Scripture for motivation. This process begins honestly with no gimmicks—just truth. Many verses apply because the Bible is crammed full of teachings on giving. One of the more familiar ones comes from Luke 6:38, which indicates that when you give, you will also receive. This verse promises that when you give, others will give to you, "pressed down, shaken together, and running over." Things will literally pour into your lap. In other words, when God gives to you, He *really* gives.

Because this is Scripture, we know it is the truth. It is God's promise so we know it will come to pass. Right? If this is true, why are so many people, who have given after hearing one of these pastoral appeals, still lacking funds? After all, they heard the truth, they responded, and then they walked out expecting a miraculous return. However, many are still waiting for the "pressed down and running over" portion to materialize.

What is the problem? Simply stated, we left them with the expectation of a miraculous answer to God's promises. Some people actually believe that if they give at church, it improves their chances of winning the lottery (which they ought to be avoiding like the plague). Some start looking in the mail for unexpected checks or yearn for a winning sweepstakes number. Of course, occasionally you may hear of someone receiving a tidy sum in that manner. However, can we agree that is not the norm for most people? And yet, the promise of return in Scripture is for every one of God's children.

Now, I like miracles. I have experienced them and seen them change many lives for the better. Still, this is not the only way God operates. What is missing? The part we have omitted is the system that God put in place for the transfer of wealth.

The Bible never indicates that the way of gaining wealth is through lotteries, sweepstakes, or unexpected windfalls. The Bible does not teach that government will care for you or that your church will be your provider. What the Bible does teach is about work, business, and God's blessing on the work of our hands.

The Bible closely connects work with God's blessings. When Jesus saw business, He blessed it. For example, look at what happened when the disciples were out fishing and having no success (see Jn. 21:3-6). Jesus told them what to do: "Cast the net on the right-hand side of the boat, and you will find some" (v. 6). Jesus knows your business, knows how to help you succeed, and—here's the best part—*wants you to succeed*. When you want the blessing of return on your giving, ask the Lord to bless the work of your hands.

Work Is Godly

There are at least three steps to the process of receiving the promise of God in response to your giving.

1. First comes the giving, a response to God stimulated by faith. Note: Action without faith is not enough.

2. In addition to giving, we must add prayer.

3. Besides giving, faith, and prayer, we must tap in to God's wealth producing system. Simply put, the secret is to find a job. Then, pray for the blessing of the Lord on that job. Ask for His creative ideas about how to do it better, receive God's strength, and complete your work in His power.

Given work's bad reputation in the church, millions have failed to seek God's blessing and presence on their work. This is a tragedy. Not only does it breed laziness and discontent at work, it fuels the "retire at 55" syndrome. In this scenario, life's prized goal becomes retiring at the very time a person has developed the experience and maturity to stabilize the workplace and mentor future leaders. Playing golf seven days a week may seem ideal, but it represents a recipe for boredom and early death. Moses wasn't lounging in the desert at 80; he was leading Israel to freedom.

A parallel development to images of early retirement is the idea of professional ministers, teachers, and praise teams "performing" for average church members. Such a scenario is not biblical. The development of marketplace ministries is challenging this concept, bringing upheaval into Christendom—which is okay. In fact, it is greatly needed. Times of change are seldom easy, but often necessary. If we don't change the status quo, we will continue to lose the momentum, power, and critical mass needed to accomplish God's mandate.

It is time to return to the plan that operated in the Old Testament and the Church in Acts. This plan is clearly spelled out in Ephesians 4:11-12, where Paul names the five gifts God gave to build up His Church. They include apostle, prophet, evangelist, pastor, and teacher.

Many are entering into long and laborious arguments about the appropriate titles for today, about which gifts are still in operation and which are not. I have been involved in those discussions many times; however, I have come to a much more practical place in my understanding. Rather than questioning titles and arguing gifts, it seems to me that we must be about the task of finding, encouraging, and equipping the modern-day Marketplace Ministers. These are the ones who are going to bring about change, and most of them could care less about what we call them. They want power, training, and encouragement to get on with the task.

Unfortunately, legions still can't accept the idea that ministry occurs outside the four walls of the church. They define "church" as a Sunday-morning gathering in a building. But this view ignores the paradigm shift taking place in the Body of Christ over the past decade.

Many have come to understand that ministry as it happened in the Bible is being restored. Not only do they believe it, they operate in structures that honor those leaders who serve outside normal church structures. Therefore, though it may not be common, it is also not atypical. Those leaders who believe in and encourage this ministry can choose whatever term they want, to refer to these ministers, as long as the Kingdom message is proclaimed.

Even though many have been slow to accept what others have seen as reality, an ever-growing body of Christians recognize that God is raising up an army of believers who are serving Him through their workplaces. Because this is such a radical departure from traditional, church-based preaching and teaching, it has taken time to catch fire. Yet, there is an expanding awareness that the Church is more than meeting in a sanctuary for training and equipping. It includes the people as they enter the community to teach others and meet needs. This is how ministry extends past the altar on Sunday.

C. Peter Wagner uses the terms "nuclear church" and "extended church" to explain this concept in a more inclusive manner. In his language, the nuclear church is the traditional group of people with a pastor, membership rolls, meeting place, and programs and activities. The extended church means members going into the world, namely, the places where they work, attend school, shop, and live the rest of the week. This language helps us identify the

Body of Christ as more than a building. It gives way to the power of ministry taking place Monday through Friday.

I wrote about this in my first book, *God@Work*; as did Ed Silvoso in *Anointed for Business*. An ever-growing list of titles on marketplace ministry appear regularly. While there have been notable forerunners, such as Dennis Peacock and Bishop Bill Hamon, this movement has gained tremendous momentum in the late 1990s and is coming into its own as a worldwide phenomenon. Os Hillman, the founder of the International Coalition of Workplace Ministries, has identified more than 1,200 such ministries in the United States alone, most which have developed in the past decade.

As profound as that number is, when I travel globally, I see that workplace ministry in Asia has moved ahead of the U.S. Individual leaders in Europe and Australia are also outpacing our nation.

Fivefold Ministries

Because of the growing acceptance of work as a place of ministry, another reality is currently taking place: recognition of the fivefold ministry in the workplace. For years, the Church operated without widely recognizing the gifts of prophet and apostle. Several years ago, the ministry of the prophetic and the office of the prophet began finding more acceptance. Today within the Body of Christ, both are widely recognized as viable ministry gifts.

In January 2004, more than 50 high-profile church leaders gathered in Orlando, Florida, at the invitation of Stephen Strang, publisher of *Ministries Today* magazine. While this summit was largely aimed at exploring matters of ethics and integrity, it is worth noting that in the position paper the group adopted, they affirmed the fivefold ministry gifts listed in Ephesians 4. Dubbed "The Orlando Statement," one of its points on these gifts noted: "We affirm that, while all of the fivefold ministries have been active since their bestowal by the ascended Christ, that the last 30 years has evidenced an increase of apostolic and prophetic ministry...."[1]

Soon after this, George Wood, general secretary of the Assemblies of God, also affirmed the existence of modern apostles and prophets in a letter to *Charisma* magazine. Commenting about an alleged dispute between Peter Wagner (profiled in an earlier issue) and some Assemblies leaders, Wood wrote, "If what is meant by modern-day apostles and prophets involves anointed persons who penetrate non-Christian environments to establish the church (apostles) and anointedly proclaim God's Word (prophets) there really is no disagreement."[2]

It is interesting to note that not only did Wood agree that apostles still exist, but that such persons penetrate non-Christian environments to establish the Church. I can't think of a better example of the activity in today's marketplace.

Because of this shift in understanding, there is a growing acceptance of the reality of these gifts in both the nuclear and extended church. As I work with, and minister to, these workplace leaders, I often recognize these fivefold gifts in operation. Occasionally, I encounter people who use the terms in speaking of their work-related endeavors.

For example, one man told me he starts all his businesses with the fivefold ministry gifts in mind. He sees himself as the apostle-visionary who starts the company. He then selects a pastor as president, who needs to oversee all the parts and make sure they operate cohesively. Next he brings in an evangelist to head the sales department. He finds a teacher to head up the training division. Finally, he identifies a prophet for each division to keep the Word of the Lord uppermost in their minds.

You may or may not agree with these definitions; someone suggested a pastor would be better suited for the human resources department than the office of president. Still, I find it fascinating that this business leader uses such a highly-defined biblical philosophy in establishing his enterprises.

While I believe that all fivefold ministry gifts are present and will become evident in the workplace, in this book I will focus on the overall ministry of marketplace leaders and will simply refer to them as "Marketplace Ministers." Wagner says, "I believe there are Apostles of Finance, Technology, Medicine, Industry, Education, the Military, and Government, Law, Communications, Business, Transportation, Nuclear Science, Agriculture and a hundred other segments of society. When these Marketplace Apostles begin to move into their rightful place under the powerful anointing of God—watch out! Revival will be right around the corner!"[3]

The simple reality is this: Most workplace ministers I know don't want to be given a title. While they don't necessarily have a theological problem with these labels, they function in a world that does not favor such terms. That is fine. People aren't effective because someone has bestowed a title on them or delivered certain prophecies over them. People function effectively because of the authority that rests upon them and the signs that follow them. The final point of the aforementioned Orlando Statement says, "We affirm the appropriation of titles by those who demonstrate the character and giftings requisite those titles, but we also affirm that the use of titles be submitted to the demands of servanthood and not become a distraction or hindrance to the very offices that they claim to serve, or the gifting they have been granted to minister."[4]

Defining Terms

As this movement gains momentum, it is creating its own vocabulary. Several years ago, when I started talking about ministry outside the local church, I used the word "marketplace" to encompass this group of ministers. My intention was to include those who weren't in a church-centered ministry, whether a businessperson, employee, schoolteacher, laborer, government worker, or housewife.

However, some observers told me the word "marketplace" did not seem to include them. Then Doug Spada, founder of the San Diego-based ministry, His Church At Work, and Os Hillman started encouraging using "workplace" as a more inclusive word.

There are still arguments on both sides of the issue. While "workplace" is more inclusive, "marketplace" has a biblical precedent as well:

> *And he went out about the third hour and saw others standing idle in the **marketplace*** (Matthew 20:3, emphasis added).

> *They are like children sitting in the **marketplace** and calling to one another, saying: "We played the flute for you, and you did not dance; we mourned to you, and you did not weep"* (Luke 7:32, emphasis added).

> *But when her masters saw that their hope of profit was gone, they seized Paul and Silas and dragged them into the **marketplace** to the authorities* (Acts 16:19, emphasis added).

While the plumber may not see his ministry in a marketplace, the chief executive officer (CEO) of a company often does not identify as clearly with "workplace" as he does with "marketplace." For my purposes, I use both words interchangeably. Since I believe there are Marketplace Ministers among plumbers and CEO's, I want to include all in this understanding.

Until now, little has been written about the specific role, qualifications, and responsibilities of Marketplace Ministers. Wagner and I recently had another conversation on this topic. Discussing who should be writing about the definitive marks of these leaders, we came up with two or three names of those who were suited for the task.

A few days later in prayer, God spoke to me, and as clearly as I can hear, He said, "Write the book." I reminded the Lord that others were more qualified and should be called on for this task. He replied that I was not His first choice, but others had not yet responded; and that if I did not do it right away, He would find someone else.

By the next day, He had shown me seven signs of a Marketplace Minister and given me a mandate to write this book quickly. I see the Marketplace Minister as not only a Christian who has a job and not just one who will occasionally tell someone about Jesus; these are men and women who see their calling to bring transformation to the world through their influence in the marketplace—that is, their sphere of influence.

When I speak of Marketplace Ministers, I am referring to the anointing and authority God gives men and women He calls to do His work. If they so choose, there are many more who can be a part of this army. Some of you reading this book will recognize yourself in this role. Others will think of a friend. Many of you will determine to take the step of faith to be a part of this powerful nation-transforming team.

No matter where you fit into this picture or where you live, I encourage you to embrace the challenge. Today is the time for you to step forth. Your workplace needs your contributions—so does your nation and world. God is calling you to set foot into the world and take His Holy Spirit with you.

Endnotes

1. "The Orlando Statement," *Ministries Today* magazine, Mar-Apr 2004, 63.

2. Letter to the editor, *Charisma* magazine, April 2004, 11.

3. C. Peter Wagner, *Apostles and Prophets* (Ventura, CA: Regal Books, 2000) 55.

4. *Ministries Today*, Mar-Apr 2004, 63.

CHAPTER 3

The Signs of a Marketplace Minister

He used the apostles and prophets for the foundation. Now He's using you, fitting you in brick by brick, stone by stone, with Christ Jesus as the cornerstone that holds all the parts together (Ephesians 2:20-21, The Message).

In the early 1980s, Bob and Bobbie Stedman joined the church that Wilma and I then pastored in San Jose, California. Owners of a thriving business, Bob and his wife both became deeply involved in the life of our church. In fact, they were so excited about their newfound faith and love of Christ they believed they should "go into ministry." When we offered Bob the position of business administrator, they sold their business and embarked on a new journey.

What started out with such passion eventually dissolved into disaster. Bobbie grew alarmed as she watched her fun-loving husband grow increasingly subdued and solemn. His problem? Trying to fit into what he conceived as the proper image of a Christian business administrator. In addition, serving in a position for which he was ill-suited created stress that negatively affected his health. Finally, it drove him to prescription drug use in search of relief.

As so often happens with medication, the pills didn't cure the problem; they masked it. Bob became increasingly dependent on medication, and his depression deepened. After nearly committing suicide, he spent three weeks in a psychiatric hospital. After his release, Bob didn't work for several months; he then picked up a temporary job as a tool truck driver.

In 1990 a friend asked Bob to go into business with him. A few months later, each established his own firm, although they maintained a close working relationship. Once again, Bob's operational skills blossomed. Finding his niche again, his business prospered and provided a good living for his family.

Then, a friend from Southern California who was starting an insurance business invited Bob and his partner to join him. Initially, it was only a part-time endeavor, with Bob devoting most of his efforts to his established business. However, God blessed this sideline until he and Bobbie were spending several days a week traveling around Northern California. Unfortunately, though, the church side of their lives wasn't going so well. Having previously attended worship services, special classes, and conferences faithfully, their travel left them feeling isolated from ministry.

Then came the Sunday in 1997 when I started a year-long series on kings and priests, emphasizing the call God places on some people to use their work as a ministry.

That message struck a chord with the Stedmans. As Bobbie recalls, "I was in the mothers' room in the back of the church with my grandbaby. I was so excited at what I was hearing I wanted to stick my head out through the window into the auditorium and shout, 'Hallelujah!' This was the answer we had been looking for. We are kings and our work is our ministry."

This talented couple is keenly aware of the responsibilities and privileges God has provided them. They recognize that the Lord owns their business and is the CEO. Wherever they travel, He creates opportunities for them to minister to others. Bob has found open doors across California, conducting business while praying for a variety of clients' and associates' needs. No one has ever rejected the offer of prayer.

"Our business has prospered and is now bringing in the finances that were once prophesied," Bobbie says. "We are blessed to have learned early on God's principles for finances and count it as one of our greatest blessings to be able to be givers on God's behalf. It is so exciting to live and daily carry out God's plan for our lives. We don't have to work at church to be good Christians. God is at work wherever we are, if we are open to His leading."

This doesn't mean the Stedmans have turned their backs on church. Today they are part of their congregation's teaching ministry, sharing the vision God has given them and encouraging people to serve God wherever they work. As Bobbie puts it, "Whatever you do, we encourage you to do it with all of your heart. Each day, ask God what He would have you do and who He would have you to touch."

The point of this story is that not everyone is cut out to serve God in a church setting. And God needs His people everywhere. As a society, we desperately need to get it right in the workplace. Businesses across the United States and around the world have been shaken by the falls of Enron, World Com, and others who have demonstrated a lack of integrity. As former Enron executive Amanda Martin put it, "In the beginning, it was brilliant, we were riding a train, we were proselytizing. We were the apostles. We were right."[1]

Despite their innate confidence, corporate merchants of greed represent counterfeits. Their claim to be apostles pales in comparison to the truth. Today's authentic ministers and nation transformers are found both in local churches and the Church in the marketplace. They seem to have similar gifts and functions, whether in the traditional church, building programs and pastoral teams, or the extended church, functioning in every element of society.

Some people emphasize the need to run the church like a business, or the reverse—running a business like a church. In fact, we don't need either scenario. I am not trying to convince business leaders to run their business like a church. What I am saying is all Christians, wherever they are, need to focus on Kingdom endeavors. Whether you are in business, government, media, science, medicine, education, homemaking, or the church, all represent Kingdom concerns. Each one is a high calling. There are visionaries in each arena. These people are modern-day Marketplace Ministers.

Marketplace Ministers

I recently had the opportunity to do some training for a wonderful Kingdom company in Barbados. This company is owned by a respected Marketplace Minister, Kyffin Simpson. He owns businesses in every Caribbean nation and territory and others in the UK and the USA. His goal in the training was not only to enhance the abilities of his managers in such skills as team building, problem solving, and conflict resolution, but to also plant deep in their hearts his own principles and values that are totally biblically based. We were able to do this in a nonthreatening way and in such language that even those who might have normally been skeptical were very receptive.

I know that this could happen only because of the impact that Mr. Simpson's life has had on his employees, and in fact, on his nation. He was recently awarded an honorary Doctorate by the University in his nation and was asked to give the graduation address. The people applauded when he said, "I am not sure that I can add anything that would be helpful for these graduates beyond what the fine professors have taught them, but I can tell you about Jesus."

In *God@Work*, the book I wrote in 2000, I observed, "In the coming revival we need to identify the apostolic leaders in the marketplace arena. God is going to begin to reveal the fivefold ministry gifts to them as they operate in the marketplace."[2] In 2002 Bill Hamon, founder of the Christian International Ministries Network, wrote *The Day of the Saints.* This book added immensely to the understanding of the role of ministers in the workplace.

If you begin a basic study of the ministry of Jesus, you will find that He started by calling men from the marketplace to work with Him. They are commonly referred to as "the Twelve." While they will always hold that distinction, they are not the only apostles mentioned in the New Testament. An inventory of those listed in Scripture includes 11 more (of which one, Junia, was a woman) and, beyond those, many unnamed apostles. It is obvious that the ministry, or gift, of the Marketplace Minister did not end with the Twelve. Now we need to determine how this affects us in the 21st century.

I served for 35 years as a pastor in a local congregational setting. During many of those years, I was under the impression that God's ministers would be primarily found in church structures. In more recent times, God has called me to minister to (and with) workplace leaders whom He is bringing to the forefront. As you might suspect, this has caused me to reexamine many of my traditional interpretations of the Bible. Now I am seeing how God has always been working in the world through people not ordinarily recognized as "professional" ministers. Through this progression of thought, I have come to accept the reality of ministers in the workplace.

We know that the Twelve original apostles were businessmen before Christ told them, "Follow Me" (Mt. 4:19). Peter was a fisherman; Matthew, a tax collector; Luke, a doctor; and so the list goes. However, certain assumptions have entered into most biblical interpretations that have caused us to miss vital distinctions. Most Bible teaching that the public receives has come from so-called professional ministers. These are the ones teaching in Bible colleges and seminaries, preaching from our pulpits, and writing the commentaries used to guide their Bible studies. By and large, this group does not see the Bible through workplace eyes. Instead, they rely on their traditional frame of reference, the nuclear church.

Not surprisingly, most of their scriptural teaching does not focus on the workplace. Look at Matthew 4:19-20, where Jesus told Peter and his brother, Andrew, " 'Follow Me, and I will make you fishers of men.' They immediately left their nets and followed Him."

When you hear a message about Peter's call to serve the Lord, it generally includes these assumptions:

1. Peter left fishing behind, a lowly calling of business, for the more prestigious calling of a full-time evangelist.

2. Peter backslid when he resumed his old lifestyle and returned to fishing after Christ's resurrection.

If you doubt me, look at this quote from a commentary on the passage John 21:3, which reads: "Simon Peter said to them, 'I am going fishing'."

Previous to the crucifixion of our Lord, the temporal necessities of himself and his disciples appear to have been supplied by the charity of individuals: Luke 8:3. As it is probable that the scandal of the cross had now shut up this source of support, the disciples, not fully knowing how they were to be employed, purposed to return to their former occupation of fishing, in order to gain a livelihood; and therefore the seven, mentioned in John 21:2, embarked on the sea of Tiberius, otherwise called the sea of Galilee.[3]

Reconsidering the Call

However, to fully understand the truth, we cannot just look at the end of the story. Instead of focusing on John 21, we must also look at the original call of the apostles. To glean another interpretation, go back to where it started. As noted above, Matthew 4:19-20 says they immediately left their nets to follow Christ. Does this mean that they left their businesses, never to return for the next three years? That they were no longer in business and that fishing was a thing of the past, subservient to the higher call of evangelism? For years this has been the most common interpretation. On closer inspection, it has several flaws:

1. *First of all, Jesus wants everyone to follow Him.*

This is foundational to the Christian faith and fundamental to all Bible-based teaching. The idea that responding to God's call means that you should automatically leave your business has caused considerable damage. Many have shed their business or occupational role to join the staff of a church or parachurch ministry. Because of prevailing thinking, they have thought this was the only way to obey God. Consequently, we have seen too many people trying to fulfill their calling in vocational ministry when that is not in their sphere of anointing.

This is a problem for the individual, since being miscast in any church role—paid or volunteer—is a prescription for burnout. It also causes complications in the corporate church, not the least of which is enormous labor costs to support a host of full-time staff members. Fortunately, the development of marketplace ministry models has reinforced the idea that some are called to serve the Lord through their businesses.

2. *The idea that Peter left his business behind him, and did not return until after the resurrection, also poses problems.*

For example, one day Jesus and Peter needed money to pay their taxes. You may recall the story from Matthew 17:25-27. Jesus instructed Peter to go and catch a fish, and he would find the exact amount of money in its mouth needed to pay the tax for both of them. Granted, this was an astonishing miracle. But no matter how you look at it, this miracle was related to Peter's business. This man fished for a living. It was as natural and ordinary as breathing and eating. So Christ chose to provide for his need through his occupation.

It is the same today. The way to gain resources—in other words, the way to get money to pay your taxes—is through work. The Lord has so much to say about work, to the point that He led

Paul to write, "For even when we were with you, we commanded you this: If anyone will not work, neither shall he eat" (2 Thess. 3:10). So it is consistent with Bible teaching that Jesus instructed Peter to obtain tax money through his work. That does not negate the power of the miracle. Instead, it enhances it.

What do I mean? If you expect that God will provide for you in unusual miracles, that may lead you to seek provision through extraordinary methods, such as a state lottery or a roulette wheel. But God is not a God of blind luck. If you can discern the miracles God performs through your work, then you can trust Him to provide you with a creative idea, a particular connection, or a masterful invention. You will obtain the resources you need. This is still a miracle, but one that occurs in the context of what God has called you to do for a living.

3. *If Peter had left his occupation behind for three years, how was he able to catch a multitude of large fish without his nets breaking when the Lord appeared after His resurrection?*

When Peter was a professional fisherman, the Lord instructed him to cast his net on the other side of the boat. When Peter did, he caught so many fish that the net began to break (see Lk. 5:6). And yet, three years later, after not being involved in the fishing business—as the commonly accepted view has been taught—he caught a huge number of fish. The Bible says that although the multitude numbered 153, the fish didn't break the net (see Jn. 21:11).

Professionally speaking, this does not make any sense. A full-time fisherman would make sure that his nets were in excellent condition. He would mend them daily and keep them in tip-top shape, always ready to head out to sea for a large catch. Yet, we have been led to believe that in a moment of weakness, Peter made a last-second decision to return to his old profession. And after a three-year absence, with his nets untended and not cared for, they were able to contain a huge catch. Pardon the pun, but does this sound a little fishy to you?

I go to these lengths to make an important point. Not only were the first apostles all businessmen, it is highly possible that some (or all) remained in business while they fulfilled their call to follow Christ. You may have heard it said that the Great Commission (see Mt. 28:18-20) command is to go into all the world and make disciples. Yet it can be more accurately stated, "As you go into all the world, make disciples." Could it be that Christ's call to follow Him is of the same genre? In other words: "Follow Me as you go about your daily tasks, which includes your work."

Marketplace Ministers

As far as we know from Scripture, the apostle Paul never left his tent-making business. I have heard some speak about Paul in this way: "He could encourage the support of others, but was never able to go into 'full-time ministry' himself. He had to continue his business on the side in order to support himself." Those who teach this imply that the business side of life constitutes a second-class profession, compared to the higher calling of full-time preaching. But as I read about Paul's ministry, his business provided an open door for sharing the gospel. Through it, he won many to Christ.

Having said this, you can see that the first apostles were not only called from the marketplace; they were also the first Marketplace Ministers. In truth, a minister in a workplace setting may be more biblical than an apostle in a nuclear church setting. (Say that too loudly in a church and you might find yourself voted out at the next business meeting!)

I don't want to focus too much on the nuclear church, but I think many would agree that modern-day churches are not exact replicas of the New Testament Church. And yet we try to fit everything into familiar operating structures. Should we be surprised that they often don't fit?

Don't get me wrong. I love the Church. I thank God for all of the new structures churches are adopting today. I praise Him for the tremendous forward strides we are taking in becoming an effective voice in the communities and nations of the world. Nevertheless, I contend that a church that recognizes that the fivefold ministry operates in the workplace, and trains its members to minister there, will be much more powerful and effective.

When I read about the modern marketplace ministry movement, I get excited. Why? Because I know God is not finished surprising us. No matter what headlines, social issues, or anti-biblical interest groups have you tied up in knots—and granted, there is plenty to be concerned about—I am still looking for a great and powerful move of God. I know that He is restoring spiritual gifts and empowering the right people to fulfill His tasks.

In his book, *The Apostolic Revolution*, David Cartledge gives a list of scriptural signs that will follow a genuine apostle, such as signs and wonders, healings, miracles, establishing local churches, suffering, visitation of angels, personal revelations of Christ, authority, sacrifices, exercising oversight and judgment, and bringing correction to churches.[4]

Cartledge goes on to explain that while Jesus is the complete model of apostolic ministry, Paul fulfilled all these signs in his life as well. This confirms that the signs of an apostle extended beyond the original Twelve; it also shows that one active in workplace ministry (like Paul) can also fulfill these signs. We will see the signs and wonders of today as the Lord uses these Marketplace Ministers to establish His Church in the workplace.

In the following chapters I will outline what I believe are the seven signs of a Marketplace Minister, which include:

1. Signs and wonders.
2. Authority.
3. Bondage breakers.
4. Wealth transfer.
5. Hearing the voice of God.
6. Biblical entrepreneurs.
7. Reaching nations.

As these signs become more apparent, they will release earth-shattering changes and victories in God's Kingdom. If you want a glimpse of the future, consider the Kingdom trends now emerging as God releases His powerful ministers in the marketplace. In his excellent book, *The God Factor*, Dr. Marcus Hester reviews an extensive list of trends he foresees unfolding in the future:

- Greater experience of wonders and miracles as the Church begins ministering outside the four walls of its buildings. People will witness increased miracles in the workplace, schools, and political settings.

- Release of grace to handle finances for God's Kingdom as wealth meant for Kingdom advances transfers to the Church. The Joseph/Daniel Company will arise to fund God's end-time harvest of souls.

- Everyday saints will assume positions as Marketplace Managers and Ministers (dual callings). The one-man ministry will cease to exist. The term "full-time ministers" will refer to the entire Body of Christ rather than a select few. Body ministry will become a normal church function.

- Financial Distribution Centers that train the Body to handle finances for the Kingdom of God will become mainstream in most evangelical churches. Cities will turn back to the Church for financial guidance as social and political needs increase.

- New positions in the Church will emerge: Ministers of Finance and Marketplace Ministers. Marketplace Apostles will be recognized in the Body of Christ just as modern-day evangelists, teachers, pastors, prophets, and territorial apostles are today. As the Church recognizes that it is in the Second Apostolic Age, God's new government will form in the nuclear church and the extended church.

- Kingdom Wisdom Centers will become mainstream in most evangelical churches. Training centers to equip marketplace leaders to minister to God's end-time harvest of souls will spring up in churches worldwide.

- Fivefold ministers will assume their roles as trainers and equippers rather than just delivering "felt need" messages. Leaders will assume their true callings (Marketplace Managers and Ministers). The Church will experience a leadership shift that will shake every fiber of its being.

- Separation of the Church and marketplace will fade away. God and His teachings will be accepted back into schools, workplaces, and politics.

- The terms "clergy" and "laity" will disappear as the saints assume roles in the Body of Christ rather than one position holding superiority. There will still be an order of spiritual authority, but the attitude that one person is better than another will cease to exist.

- Christians will assume new leadership roles in the political, social, business, and military realms. The God factor will be socially accepted as a legitimate tool for solving problems in society and the workplace.

- City transformation will occur. Whole cities will experience revival and turn toward God. Miracles that occurred in the Book of Acts will become commonplace again.

- The fear of the Lord will become real in many people's lives. While Christians will experience great persecution, more people will become Christians than at any time in history.

- Prayer intercessors will emerge in the marketplace. The need for prayer covering and strategic prayer plans for businesses will become as normal as prayer for churches and their leaders are today. Marketplace intercessors will not only cover businesses but will train others to pray for the release of wealth and souls in the marketplace.

- Personal testimonies from the Body of Christ will become a major ingredient perpetuating the marketplace ministry movement. Accounts of how God is working in people's lives will release great faith to the rest of the Church to help fulfill their dual calling in this movement.[5]

Are you ready to see such incredible things happen? Read on for the seven signs of those who will help usher in this age of blessing.

Endnotes

1. Bethany McLean and Peter Elkind, *The Smartest Guys in the Room* (New York: The Penguin Group, 2003) 38.

2. Rich Marshall, *God@Work* (Shippensburg, PA: Destiny Image Publishers, 2000) 124.

3. While *Adam Clarke's Commentary* was published in 1826, and thus is in the public domain, this reference came from *Bible Explorer*, published by WORDsearch Corp., Austin, Texas, electronic database, copyright 1999.

4. David Cartledge, *The Apostolic Revolution* (Chester Hill, NSW, Australia: Paraclete Institute, 2000) 265-266.

5. Dr. Marcus Hester, *The God Factor* (Shippensburg, PA: Treasure House, division of Destiny Image Publishers, 2003) 173-175.

CHAPTER 4

Signs and Wonders

All the signs that mark a true apostle were in evidence when I was with you through both good times and bad: signs of portent, signs of wonder, signs of power (2 Corinthians 12:12, The Message).

Larry Ihle and Dick Hochreiter are two Marketplace Ministers I have encountered during my worldwide travels the past six years. They obediently go to various places as God leads them, all the while doing the same work as Paul accomplished nearly 2,000 years ago.

Larry runs a dental laboratory business in Farmington, Minnesota. Dick, who lives near Palm Springs, California, formerly ran a company that manufactured motorcycle apparel. He now operates The Prayer Company, which produces various anointing oils and other products to encourage prayer and witnessing in the world. This pair of business ministers do God's work in Albania, Thailand, the Philippines, Argentina, and closer to home. Whatever the location, miracles follow them. They believe in the power of Jesus to do what He said He would do, so they pray, expecting that people will be healed and that unusual signs will accompany them.

One time we were together in Manila. Former businessman and evangelist Ed Silvoso and I had traveled there to speak at a conference on the theme of reaching cities for Christ. While we discussed this topic, Larry, Dick, and Scott Kilber—a pastor who often travels and ministers with them—were in the hotel doing the work of Marketplace Apostles.

One day on the elevator they met the hotel manager, also an American. After introducing themselves and explaining why they were there, they asked the manager if he had any prayer needs. Shaking his head, he replied, "Just that you pray for the television system to start working again." Not only had it quit, but repairmen estimated it would take two weeks to get it back in operation. As you might suspect, many guests were irate. Larry nodded and said, "Okay, we'll go pray about that."

After they went to their room, Larry said, "I honestly wouldn't mind if the cable system stayed down for awhile. But we asked the manager if he had any needs, and his need is for the cable system to come up. So we'll pray about that." An hour later, the manager called their room to thank them for his request being answered; the cable system was back on line and operating fine. He concluded, "If you need anything, just let me know."

Larry said to Dick, "I do need something; I need to lead him to the Lord."

Going to his office, they knocked on the door.

"Come right in," the manager said, smiling. "What do you need?"

"I need to tell you how that cable TV system got fixed," Larry said. "We prayed to the God of the universe who fixed it. He loves you so much that He would do that for you. Would you like to know Him?"

"Yes, please."

So, they proceeded to explain the gospel and the sacrifice Christ made for him. Not only did the manager accept Jesus as Savior and Lord, but before that conference concluded, Larry, Dick, and Scott also led more than three dozen employees to Christ. I tell folks that Ed Silvoso and I led a conference, but these men performed signs and wonders. Before our stay ended, these new converts decided to start a church in the hotel and selected the restaurant manager to be their pastor, who had been a Christian before backsliding. That week he had rededicated his life to God.

These new Christians had to get their new pastor's girlfriend in a right relationship with God, too, and persuade them to get married. The couple had been living together, and the church didn't want their pastor in an adulterous relationship. When I share this story, it invariably provokes protests. Christians start airing their theological objections and say, "That guy can't pastor the church." Yes, he can. To these people, he was the most spiritually mature person available.

When Larry and Dick mentioned to Ed that they had asked the people if they had ever been baptized, Silvoso said, "You don't ask them about baptism. you tell them what they need to do. You're their leaders. You're their ministers. Tell them what they need." When they relayed this message to these new Christians, the people agreed to be baptized. However, the three Americans had a flight to catch at 7 a.m. the next morning. So the people said, "Fine, we'll meet you at five o'clock."

"Okay, meet us at the pool," Larry said.

The next morning, everyone showed up dressed for work in their usual attire—tuxedos, restaurant finery, and the like. Nobody had any standard baptismal gear, thus this situation demanded immediate improvisation. Most evangelical Christians who insist on baptism by immersion would have tossed them into the pool in their tuxedos (great for fidelity to Scripture, but not too practical for reporting to work as soon as the ceremony ends).

What happened next would likely upset many church leaders. But if you believe that the most important concern is a person's heart, you may be able to appreciate it. Larry and Dick decided they could baptize people by immersion and at the same time not get their clothes wet. All they had to do was find a large bowl, fill it with water, and immerse these converts' faces in the bowl. Thank God for creative businesspeople who can find solutions. In a workplace setting, meeting needs comes before demanding tradition be upheld.

God@Work

Larry has shared other stories of God's power. He and Dick regularly visit businesses to pray for the owners, and the owners often invite them back to pray for their employees. Larry does this at his own business, with a daily morning prayer session at 10 o'clock. Although optional, customarily a third of the employees show up. (Nearly all of them came the morning after the September 11 terrorist attacks in 2001.) In fact, he has traced the dramatic increases in profitability that his 28-year-old company has seen recently, to the intercessors who started praying for his firm in 1994.

Once, when they were experiencing financial difficulties, a prayer warrior called Larry to say that he had a vision of a black hand dipping into a pot. That sparked an investigation that led to the discovery of theft by an employee, which otherwise would probably have gone undetected.

Larry says this corporate prayer program has returned dividends far beyond monetary ones. Once, en route to a meeting in London, he sensed that he should pray for the dentists and suppliers he was meeting, an action he later shared with the group. There were 300 dentists in this association, each of them with a family and approximately 1,500 patients. So as Larry saw it, God had given him a potential congregation of 450,000 members. Now, when dentists send prescriptions for crowns, partial plates, or other equipment, they often include prayer requests with the order.

This activity does not just occur in his office. During the construction of Larry's new home, he led 57 subcontractors and workers to accept Christ as Savior. Four people were healed. Some of them now attend meetings he holds there most Monday nights, teaching others how to take God's Word into the marketplace.

"My point has never been to get wealth," Larry says of the amazing developments in his business-based ministry. "You bring the Kingdom of God into your business, and things are set free. Say you were in the computer industry and had access to Bill Gates; he gave you his personal cell phone number and said, 'If you need anything, don't hesitate to call.' Would you rather have that or the One who created Bill Gates?"

I could go on, but you get the idea. Where does such power and authority come from? From God-confirming ministry with signs and wonders. The miracles of a workplace minister may not be the same ones that we have seen in the local church, but they still open the doors for the Word of God to spread and for souls to come into His Kingdom. As with that hotel in Manila, in the days ahead, we will see more workplace churches planted, companies restored, and nations touched by God's power.

This is similar to the description another Marketplace Minister, Paul, gave about the power of the Lord in his life and ministry: "I have won them over by the miracles done through me as signs from God—all by the power of God's Spirit. In this way, I have fully presented the good news of Christ all the way from Jerusalem clear over into Illyricum." (See Romans 15:19 NLT.)

A discussion of workplace ministers starts with signs and wonders. This is the clearest biblical sign God gives to His children. The one sign by which the apostle Paul wanted his ministry judged was its ability to bring the life-changing grace of Jesus Christ to men. This is what he said: "When I was with you, I certainly gave you every proof that I am truly an apostle, sent to you by God Himself.

For I patiently did many signs and wonders and miracles among you" (2 Cor. 12:12 NLT).

Workplace Miracles

If we accept Christ's words as true, the question becomes, "What kind of miracles will Marketplace Apostles do?" The answer is, "All kinds." In John 14:12, Jesus made it clear that whatever He had done, we could do even greater things. Jesus performed miracles that met the needs of those He was ministering to:

- When they were sick, He healed them.

- If they were hungry, He gave them food.

- When the bridegroom needed wine at the wedding in Cana, He provided it.

Recently, a businessman told me, "I know that I am not anointed with authority in the marketplace because I do not see miracles like Jesus did." Well, not all miracles of today will look exactly like the ones that Jesus did. He didn't say that we would do exactly what He had done, but that we would do greater things.

Many people automatically equate miracles with healings. But today, life expectancy is much greater than in New Testament times, and medical knowledge is far more advanced. The potential of healing coming through such natural means of God's provision is quite high. Although I still expect to see healings (in fact, many), I have set my sights on greater things. In Romans 15:19, when Paul confidently and boldly stated his call, he spoke of mighty signs and wonders accomplished by the power of God's Spirit.

A sign is that which distinguishes one person from another. A sign in the workplace is confirmation from God that you are following His agenda. A sign could be a marketing idea or a prophetic look into the future. It could be a word from the Lord that opens new venues for sales. Or, it could be a warning that keeps you out of trouble. A sign will be God's answer to your need. So look for signs in the areas of need.

When Dick and Larry were in the Philippines, they prayed for the cable TV system to come back on, although personally they may have preferred that it remain off. However, this was the manager's need. Meeting it became the doorway to his conversion and that of dozens of employees.

Likewise, the signs of a Marketplace Minister—indications that God is on your side—will fit the area of whatever needs are particular to your business. It may well be that you will find yourself praying for the sick and seeing them recover. But if your signs are in another area, it does not mean that you are not working with mighty power and wonders.

The goal is effectiveness. In a church setting, the reality of Christ's gospel is not seen in the size of a local congregation, its building, or the number of programs it offers. The evidence comes not in the size of the offerings or the quality of its music, but through the number of changed lives. If there are no changed lives, the ministry is not successful. As a pastor, I know that the focus of many churches is numbers, be it people, money, or the size of the building. However, in reviewing the spread of the gospel in recent decades, better measurements must be used.

For example, when I started preaching 40 years ago, a commonly reported statistic was that one of every two marriages in our nation ended in divorce. Yet inside the church only one of 50 were breaking apart. Christianity made a difference in marriage. If you needed help with yours, going to church was a wise choice. Yet, Promise Keepers recently produced a video that stated the divorce rate among Christians is equal to, or possibly greater than, the rest of the population.

Obviously, our current methods of dealing with marital situations aren't working too well. There must be a change, which must include the power of God. We need divine intervention and signs and wonders to reverse this dreadful situation. The same is true in the marketplace. We are looking for evidence of the power of God and His stamp of approval on what we are doing.

One of the ways God does this is by providing ideas and methods that will produce results, such as higher sales or meeting or exceeding profit projections. However, there must be more. Now, I do not downplay the importance of profitability. I believe God wants His children to prosper. He gives a level of authority in your community that stems from this kind of success. I want that for you as well, since I see it as one of God's signs.

Still, there must be a spiritual dimension to business. I'm talking about the tangible presence of God—that peace that comes from knowing His power is there and available at any moment. Knowing that you can hear from God in the midst of a business deal gives you a sense of power. Confidence comes from knowing He is on your side. Peace comes from knowing that any obstacles you, your customers, and your competitors face can be handled by the power of God.

Expect God to be present with signs and wonders. Expect that when you encounter sickness, it will be healed. Expect to speak to the frustrated, the lonely, the depressed, and the discouraged. Anticipate seeing God work in their lives. Raise your level of expectation to include answers to business problems, God's intervention in sealing business deals, and His confirmation through tangible goals that are a mark of success.

Confirming Signs

A clear biblical sign of an apostle, or a Marketplace Minister, comes through signs and wonders, both the spiritual variety and in earthly means. Let's look first at the biblical basis.

> In mighty signs and wonders, by the power of the Spirit of God, so that from Jerusalem and round about to Illyricum I have fully preached the gospel of Christ (Romans 15:19).

> And my speech and my preaching were not with persuasive words of human wisdom, but in demonstration of the Spirit and of power, that your faith should not be in the wisdom of men but in the power of God (1 Corinthians 2:4-5).

For the kingdom of God is not eating and drinking, but righteousness and peace and joy in the Holy Spirit. For he who serves Christ in these things is acceptable to God and approved by men (Romans 14:17-18).

And then the lawless one will be revealed, whom the Lord will consume with the breath of His mouth and destroy with the brightness of His coming. The coming of the lawless one is according to the working of satan, with all power, signs, and lying wonders, and with all unrighteous deception among those who perish, because they did not receive the love of the truth, that they might be saved. And for this reason God will send them strong delusion, that they should believe the lie (2 Thessalonians 2:8-11).

Mighty deeds are those that exhibit strength, power, and ability. Ultimately, this discussion boils down to faith, which is the foundation for believing in signs and wonders. Absolute trust in God must be a constant theme in the life of a workplace minister. The late Smith Wigglesworth (who, by the way, was a plumber) is widely known in Christian circles as "The Apostle of Faith." Wigglesworth emphasized belief in the fact that God could do the impossible. As he exercised great faith in what God could do, the Lord did great things through him.[1]

In my interactions with workplace leaders around the world, I see recurring examples of faith presenting themselves as the basis for the miracles, signs, and remarkable "God events." Whatever your marketplace endeavor, I encourage you to seek God until He provides a specific revelation for your situation. Trusting in the Holy Spirit to guide you, allow that inward revelation to move you to a position of steadfastness, being immovable and abounding in God's work. As First John 2:27 says, "But the anointing which you have received from Him abides in you, and you do not need that anyone teach you; but as the same anointing teaches you concerning all things, and is true, and is not a lie, and just as it has taught you, you will abide in Him."

A simple definition of anointing is the supernatural empowerment of God that allows you to do things through Him that you could not do on your own.

Some might ask, "What do you mean by 'things that you could not do on your own'? Even Jesus said, 'I can do nothing on My own.' "

That I understand, but it is still the truth that you can do many things through the power of the flesh or your natural abilities. You need the anointing of God, however, to move into the supernatural. This is the arena where God's power and ability make the difference, not yours. This is what we need in our lives today—the power to accomplish feats through God's anointing.

Even though *anointing* is most often used in church settings, that is not its biblical context. First John 2:27 says the anointing is for "all things." It is God's anointing that enables humans to move into supernatural strength. That anointing abides, or lives, in you. If it lives in you, then when you go to work, God's anointing is there.

This verse also tells us that we don't need a teacher to allow God to work through us. There are things that God can, and wants, to do for you that cannot be learned in a training seminar, conveyed in a manual, or obtained through on-the-job training. These are the things that only God can do and He loves doing them for us. Think back over your own life and recall the times that God came through at exactly the right moment. He can do this all the time, and He wants to do it again today.

We must stir up our faith for signs and wonders in the workplace. Some will have to do with work, some with coworkers, and some with creative ideas for the future. While it is not necessarily simple to sort out His direction, this much I know: If your faith gets in line with God's ability, you will see tangible results.

Endnote

1. Smith Wigglesworth, *Smith Wigglesworth on the Holy Spirit* (New Kensington, PA: Whitaker House, 1998) 9.

CHAPTER 5

Authority

You may think I overstate the authority He gave me, but I'm not backing off. Every bit of my commitment is for the purpose of building you up, after all, not tearing you down (2 Corinthians 10:8, The Message).

A few years ago, a friend of mine had a business idea that he wanted Gunner Olson to consider. He invited me to the meeting, but the proposal soon took a backseat in my mind. Within a few seconds of meeting Olson for the first time, I was left with a lasting impression of this kindhearted Swede. When he spoke, I wanted to shout back, "Yes, sir!" even though he was addressing someone else. His authoritative voice and considerable presence commanded a hearing. While I am sure that he exhibits many other signs of a Marketplace Minister, what stands out in my mind is his authority.

The founder of the International Christian Chamber of Commerce (ICCC), Olson is making an impact on all continents of the world. Perhaps the most notable examples are the Chamber's educational outreaches in China and connections it has forged with business leaders in Israel. These are fascinating projects.

Despite its official communist policies, China is experiencing dramatic changes, including expanding Christian influence across the nation, as chronicled recently by former *Time* magazine bureau chief David Aikman in his book, *Jesus in Beijing: How Christianity Is Transforming China and Changing the Global Balance of Power.* The ICCC has seen reality of this, too. Several years ago, the government invited the organization to film a ten-part series on entrepreneurship titled, "You Can Start a Business." Writing the curriculum, ICCC's training division used biblically based principles as the foundation of the series. Although not allowed to use direct references to the Bible or Jesus, narrators would say, "It is written" before introducing a chamber member who delivered a talk on how following a certain principle aided his business.

These teaching tapes were so well received they have been broadcast on the nation's second largest television network (a potential viewing audience of 40 million) and adapted for use in 165 government-owned distance education learning centers. By mid-2003, more than 42,000 college-age students had viewed it. The ten-part series is being expanded to 30 lessons, with a second series, "Developing a Leading Business," scheduled to become an accredited, university course.

ICCC is also building bridges with Israeli businessmen, in spite of the fact that this development doesn't attract the kind of news coverage that conflict and charges of anti-Semitism generate. This operation began a few years ago with a process designed to create new opportunities for Israeli merchants. These beleaguered business owners were suffering from the triple plague of continuing terrorism, decreased tourism, and a worldwide economic slump.

In the summer of 2002, with members in some 90 nations, ICCC brought a delegation to meet with Israeli officials and businesspersons. This wasn't a specifically Christian initiative. Instead, its purpose was to fulfill God's command to show this nation Christ's love. Not only did this result in 1,100 face-to-face discussions about potential business deals, but Olson also spoke at a banquet that week attended by 200 top business leaders. The audience included such people as a software developer who had sold one of his companies to AOL for $450 million, CEOs of leading corporations, and other giants of industry. Not only did Olson's remarks draw a standing ovation, the ICCC delegation received an invitation to return later that year for a "solidarity conference" organized by the prime minister.

In his autobiography, *Business Unlimited*, Olson tells of once being asked to address a crowd of 3,000 in Africa. The audience included the nation's president, deputy secretary general of the United Nations, ministers of finance from the Ivory Coast, and other high-ranking officials. Unprepared to speak, on his way to the podium he remembered a dream his first night in Benin. In the dream, he wandered endlessly through villages in the nation's interior. Everyone he met had no face. He interpreted the sudden recall of this dream as a signal from the Holy Spirit to speak from his heart. Olson writes:

" 'Last night I had a strange dream,' I began. 'I saw the faceless people of Benin, who were born with nothing, who are nobodies. Thousands of them. They seem to be a people without a future, and yet some of them are carrying the future of their nation. Those are the people we have come to serve. Those people are the future of Benin; they are the wealth of the nation. That's why we're here. We're here to serve the faceless people of Benin. Whatever we're doing, if it doesn't reach them, then what we're doing is in vain. They are so loved by God and they're precious to Him.' "[1]

Later, Olson recalls, "There in Benin, I was again glimpsing that vital principle—that as we are faithful in the small things, God gives us bigger projects. Everything we do is to the glory of His name to accomplish His Kingdom on earth. Whatever happens, it's through the love and grace of God rather than anything we do ourselves. Without Him, I am nothing. I am like one of those faceless people of my dream."[2]

Powerful Word

Authority! There is something strong about the word. It brings to mind power. In fact, most of the time, that is the way the original Greek is translated in the New Testament. As the apostle Paul understood his authority, so will the modern-day Marketplace Minister. After signs and wonders, authority is the second characteristic of such leaders.

"Authority," as it appears in Second Corinthians 10:8, refers to the power of choice, the liberty to do as one pleases. It also speaks of physical and mental power, and the ability or strength with which one is vested, possesses, or exercises. In addition, it refers to the power of authority (influence) and of right (privilege), or the power of rule or government. The Greek root is talking about the power wielded by a person whose will and commands bring obedience and submission. On a personal level, it speaks of one who possesses authority, such as a ruler or magistrate. Significantly, for our consideration, *Strong's Concordance* of the Bible says it is the sign of regal authority—a crown.

I opened this chapter with a modern paraphrase of Second Corinthians 10:8. The New King James Version reads, "For even if I should boast somewhat more about our authority, which the Lord gave us for edification and not for your destruction, I shall not be ashamed." In whatever version you prefer, there are three points that stand out about Paul's authority:

1. *He obviously understood its scope.*

Many thought he was overstating it, making it bigger and more powerful than he should have. But he tells them, "I am not ashamed," or as Eugene Peterson puts it in *The Message*, "I am not backing off." When God's authority resides in you, there is no backing down. Divine authority brings with it a boldness that cannot be diminished or turned aside.

2. *Paul knew the source of his authority.*

He simply says, "God gave it to me." This is not the kind of authority that stems from being born in a powerful family, elected to a certain position, earning a string of educational degrees, or some other source of man's choosing. It is delegated by God.

3. *He understood the purpose of the authority.*

Unlike human authority that often seeks to glorify the powerful or boast about lording it over others, Paul didn't exercise authority for himself. Instead, it was for the good of the people. Marketplace Ministers also know how to use authority. They understand its scope, its source, and its purpose.

Many people would search for such ministers among the CEOs and business owners of a city. While many of them may fit this category, I believe that God is installing His influential ministers wherever they are needed. Therefore, we will find them at many levels of business, government, education, law, and other organizations. Since this authority is God-given, it is not limited to those we would delegate it to, based on human reasoning. One of the most noticeable and truest signs for marketplace transformation is authority.

Authority can be delegated, such as the authority of a policeman, security guard, or federal marshal. However, such agents' authority is only evident when they are on the job, or in off-duty roles while wearing a uniform. There is a difference with divinely appointed authority, like the type referred to by Paul and present in Marketplace Ministers. While it is also delegated authority, it is delegated by God; and therefore, it carries a legal right to be exercised *whenever it is needed.*

Marketplace authority also looks different from the authority present in the nuclear church, where leaders oversee church structures and plans. It is the kind of authority that rests on a person so powerfully it causes others to respond whenever the minister speaks. This can happen in a union meeting, during a coffee break, at a board meeting, or amid a seemingly casual conversation. The authority has an innate quality of making itself known.

A unique "Kingdom authority" operates in the business arena. Therefore, while seen in business dealings, it will also be evident in

God's activity in cities and regions. Ultimately, this will lead to societal transformation. This authority will operate in the true sense of "the elders that sit in the gates," a position of honor that was held by the husband of the Proverbs 31 woman (see Prov. 31:23).

To date, this has been the kind of position that has rested exclusively in the hands of pastors and leaders in the nuclear church. However in the new paradigm, the gatekeepers—those voices of authority in cities and nations with regard to spiritual insight—will largely belong to Marketplace Ministers. Of course, the awesome woman in Proverbs also had her place in the gates (see v. 31). So we need to be ready to expand our understanding to include both men and women in the workplace as those who will carry the authority to change the future.

The Kingdom authority possessed by Marketplace Ministers carries with it an anointing for governmental-type authority. When Proverbs 31 refers to those who sit in the gates, it is talking about the place where decisions are made that affect the entire city. It speaks of the place where legal transactions occur, as well as financial and other decisions affecting the local population's direction and destiny.

We see this in the parable that Jesus tells in Luke 19:12-27. In this story, Jesus teaches businesspeople about gaining authority in their city. He tells them that doing business in such a way that they create great financial gain will also yield authority in their city and surrounding areas. (It concludes that there is potential for authority in ten cities, which may or may not be geographically connected.) The authority that Christ speaks of is the same authority that Paul claims God has given to him. It is authority that gives jurisdiction in cities.

Kingdom Cash

We need to start thinking about authority outside traditional interpretations—and not just who can exert authority, but the tools that go with it. For example, consider money. For years, especially in the church world, it has borne the image of "filthy lucre." Yet, money is a tool God gives to businesspersons to gain authority in their city—that means money to carry out tasks that will benefit society, not just a particular church or ministry.

Viewing money in this way can adjust our perspective, making it a powerful tool for building God's Kingdom. But think of it as Kingdom money, not church money. Not project money, or ministry money, but Kingdom money. Kingdom money carries the potential for carrying great authority with it.

Consider what Kingdom money is and the power it includes. The Bible has much to say about money. You may be surprised to learn that it has more to say about money than faith or even salvation. According to Earl Pitts and Craig Hill, coauthors of *Wealth, Riches and Money*: "The New Testament actually contains 215 verses pertaining to faith, 218 verses pertaining to salvation, and 2,084 verses dealing with stewardship of, and accountability for, money and finance."[3] Through His Word, God wants to teach us to understand the concepts of money and the purposes behind it.

Cash is an overpowering force in many people's lives. Most think a lot about money. They work for it and dream about getting truckloads of it. Many gamble away small fortunes in the vain hope of hitting an elusive jackpot. Money can become an all-consuming idol when it dominates our thought life and actions. Sadly, if most polls are accurate, the only reason the majority of people work is to gain money. With this kind of focus, the goal of work is to get enough money to stop working and enjoy the benefits money can buy. But they're never really satisfied, because no matter how much they have, it will never be enough.

The question is: Why did Jesus talk so much about money? Was it because He knew how important it would be to us? Or did He have deeper motives and purposes? On one occasion He warned sternly against craving it: "No one can serve two masters; for either he will hate the one and love the other, or else he will be loyal to the one and despise the other. You cannot serve God and mammon" (Mt. 6:24).

In some versions of the Bible, the word "mammon" is translated as "money." But to quote Pitts and Hill: "Let's begin by talking about the meaning of the above-quoted passage in Matthew 6. To what is Jesus referring when He uses 'Mammon'? Firstly, it is important to see that whatever mammon is, Jesus places it in a position that is diametrically opposed to God. It is anti-God. Whatever mammon is competes with God to be served.

"When He said that the two, God and mammon, could not both be served, Jesus was not speaking about a prohibition against such, but rather an impossibility of doing such. Jesus was not stating, 'It would be wrong to try to serve both God and mammon,' but rather, 'It is impossible to serve both God and mammon.' God and mammon are opposites, and thus cannot both be served at the same time. Serving one categorically precludes serving the other. Thus, either God or mammon can only be served exclusively. In order to truly serve God, one must totally renounce mammon and have nothing at all to do with it."[4]

As you contemplate money and mammon, think about this truth: If they are the same thing, then we must have nothing whatsoever to do with money. In fact, some Christians have taken this view and consider poverty to be synonymous with holiness. But even for those who have supposedly taken a vow to remain poor, they still need some money to exist.

I don't believe that money and mammon are the same thing. Yet, getting this concept firmly planted in our minds will help us understand the power of Kingdom authority that can be exercised through money. Mammon is more likely a spirit. It is an evil spirit that causes people to focus unhealthy amounts of attention on money. When this happens, money becomes the goal. But God wants us to have Him as our goal.

In reality, money has no power in and of itself. It is the source of the money that has power. Jesus is telling us that the source will either be God or mammon. When the true power behind your financial provision is God, then you have the potential of achieving Kingdom authority through your money. If you derive your money through greed, avarice, or illegal or immoral transactions, you will lack the power and the authority that God wants to give you.

Simply put, if you spend almost all your time thinking about money, it is very likely that the spirit of mammon has a grip on your life. On the other hand, when you spend most of your time thinking about God and His ability and desire to provide for your needs—and wholesome purposes it can accomplish, such as feeding the hungry or clothing the needy—you are ready to step into Kingdom authority.

So for a Marketplace Minister, one avenue for gaining authority is through the acquisition of money. However, it is not the money that gives the authority; it is God. So just having a lot of money does not guarantee the kind of authority that Jesus is referring to in Luke 19. (And, in fact, there are other avenues to gain the authority that the Lord wants to give His followers.)

Where Does Money Go?

Still, money is a crucial issue when it comes to operating with Kingdom authority. Where does a Marketplace Minister use his money? To date, most spiritual leaders have called for a person of authority to fund major building projects and mission endeavors associated with his or her church. There may have been a challenge to move beyond the local assembly to a regional, national, or international project; but the emphasis usually goes on retaining funds within a nuclear church model.

However, in order to exert authority in a city, there must be some way that the city benefits. Even before this, there must be some way for the city to recognize the authority via the resource that rests in the hands of the Marketplace Minister. I do not believe that an ostentatious lifestyle is necessary to establish such authority.

Yet, I believe that it must be obvious to those in the city that God's blessing is behind this person's provisions.

A city has needs that must be addressed by Marketplace Ministers if they are to have authority there. Previously, most of God's ministers have operated in a sphere of authority that extends only within a tiny area of influence. Ordinarily, this has been confined to the church structure with which the person identifies—local church first, followed by regional or national denomination, overseer, or network. Marketplace Ministers must operate outside of conventional, nuclear church models. Therefore, they must be ready to expend considerable resources on activities that appear to have no Christian connection. (I will deal with this in more detail in the next chapter on the sign of breaking bondages.)

For years we have attempted to reach cities by means of nuclear church programs, outreaches, church planting, unity efforts, prayer movements, and every other conceivable local church concept. Yet, when Jesus speaks of authority in the city, He is referring to the impact that comes from businesspeople doing business. I am confident that when Marketplace Apostles are recognized for who they are, we will see new strategies and actions that will result in major, beneficial changes in the cities and nations of the world.

Before closing this chapter, I need to emphasize that money is only one means of gaining authority for a Marketplace Apostle. Authority in a city or a nation also comes through political means, media, and wisdom. Sometimes God simply gives a level of authority that others respond to, yet it has an identifiable source. Being the Lord, God sometimes just does things that we cannot understand. In other words, it is possible for someone who does not have great financial resources to carry high levels of authority. Governmental offices and key positions in broadcasting and print media will open doors for many in the future.

We can start to identify these ministers to the workplace as we see the level of city, area-wide, regional, and national authority surfacing. We will see these ministers in all arenas. And no matter what we call them, they will operate with the authority of the Lord on their lives.

Endnotes

1. J. Gunnar Olson, *Business Unlimited* (Orebro, Sweden: International Christian Chamber of Commerce, 2002) 12.

2. Ibid, 13.

3. Craig Hill and Earl Pitts, *Wealth Riches and Money* (Littleton, CO: Family Foundations Publishing, 2001) 3.

4. Ibid, 13-14.

CHAPTER 6

Bondage Breakers

What shall we say then? Is there unrighteousness with God? Certainly not! (Romans 9:14)

"Hope for the City." While that is an appropriate name for the ministry to needy residents of Minneapolis and St. Paul, Minnesota, it could be renamed "Hope for the World." What started as an effort to donate surplus equipment and goods to inner-city ministries has expanded into a worldwide outreach that in 2003 distributed more than $300 million worth of goods. This included shipments of AIDS medications to Africa, hospital equipment to North Korea, vaccinations to Indonesia, and food and clothing to Afghanistan.

During its first year of operations in 2000, Hope for the City distributed items valued at $2 million. That means that in four years this ministry saw more than a hundredfold increase, like the kind Christ described in Mark 4:20. What started as a modest effort to make use of excess warehouse space managed by a real estate company turned into a multinational endeavor that attracted donations from such well-known companies as The Gap, Old Navy, Wal-Mart, Office Depot, Bed Bath & Beyond, and Avon.

Hope for the City is the brainchild of Dennis and Megan Doyle, owners of the Welsh Companies, Minnesota's largest full-service real estate firm. While the company manages more than 22 million square feet of real estate valued at $1.5 billion, Dennis derives considerable delight from the ministry side of his endeavors: "I get more meaning from shipping a container of blankets into Afghanistan and saving lives than doing another real estate deal."

The Doyles are living examples of Marketplace Ministers. These leaders use their authority and expertise to do more than make money. Their impressive accomplishment with Hope for the City didn't come overnight; it started a decade ago with a weekly prayer meeting in the Doyles' suburban home. Megan says they started praying after her husband had utilized every natural ability and gift and failed to succeed.

"We felt our business needed prayer like everyone needs prayer," says Megan, noting that the company hired a staff member as a full-time intercessor for two years, along with an administrative assistant who filled the role of pastor. "We pray for every developer, employee, spouse, and family. Most businesspeople don't understand they can apply the principles they learn on Sunday on Monday."

As to why God is moving so mightily today in the workplace, Dennis attributes it to a redefining of church in the 21st century. "For many years that was commonly associated with a place you went on Sundays, when in reality first-century believers carried the church's influence wherever they traveled. Christians have focused considerable attention on their sanctuaries when the most meaningful activity takes place in the outside world," he says.

"We've all tried very hard to do prayer events and bring pastors together and bring revival; and it's not worked out very well," Dennis comments. "Real authority is outside the church. We need the whole Body of Christ working together if we're going to see revival in the United States. I think God is saying, 'If it's going to happen, it's going to be in the marketplace.' "

However, the Doyles aren't the only business-based Marketplace Ministers in the Twin Cities. Attorney Jay Bennett and his wife, Sally, have worked individually—and in cooperation with the Doyles—to attack the problems of poverty, hunger, drug addiction, prostitution, and loneliness that plague their area.

Several years ago, Bennett used his background in corporate law to create Kingdom Oil, a networking ministry that creates partnerships between business and faith leaders. By joining pools of money, talent, and prayer, Kingdom Oil is striving to improve its community and give people hope.

This isn't some vague concept to throw money at problems. Bennett thinks of it as a spiritual investment bank. A syndicate of investors forms relationships with ministries and helps equip them for their tasks. This includes showing ministries ways of developing and refining the skills needed to manage their endeavors. Organized under rules for a Christian foundation, Kingdom Oil has nine "portfolios" promoting compassion and justice.

"Our vision is the Twin Cities as God's Kingdom, and our mission is to proclaim and network that vision until it becomes reality," Bennett says. "Jesus taught us that the Kingdom is at hand, and that teaching has never changed. I view my law firm as a place of ministry. The marketplace is where we can demonstrate the gospel by living out what we proclaim. We can use our gifts to serve our neighbor and change our community so that it looks more like what the Lord intends. I try to get people to view work as sacred. When a businessperson grasps that, embraces that, and starts living it out, everything changes. Work becomes much more fun and compelling.

"I see a progressive, powerful awakening where leaders are realizing they have been placed in a powerful spot for ministry. Artificial barriers like church and state don't need to exist. Faith-based ministries offer the opportunities that traditional welfare and government efforts haven't met. But our history has been so isolated and scattered. The church has to form a strategic plan that's bigger than any one person or business."

To draw an analogy to the past, Bennett compares the task to America's network of nationwide railroads developed in the 1800s. Central Pacific and Union Pacific had two major routes that didn't intersect until the government said, "You're going to meet in Utah." Likewise, the Church needs to provide an intersection between faith in Christ and the rest of society: "I think a lot of people will come to Christ through the Second Commandment to love our neighbor. A lot of people will understand the First Commandment about loving God as they learn to love their neighbor."

Transforming Society

Why would a successful real estate executive and a highly regarded attorney even care about social problems, much less do anything about them? Because decay and injustice must be resolved. I believe the leaders in this necessary effort for social transformation will be the marketplace leaders whom God is calling out in every city and nation around the world.

"Justice" and "righteousness" are closely connected in the Bible and mean nearly the same thing. They are surely on God's heart, but when Paul discusses them in the ninth chapter of Romans you can almost hear the cry of the apostle's heart as well. He talks about righteousness and moves on to God's compassion, reminding us that God will show compassion on whomever He chooses. Then Paul adds a note about God's mercy and power. Can you see the progression, from righteousness to justice, compassion, mercy, and power? When people come against injustice, and add God's compassion and mercy, they create a recipe for power.

Some may say, "We have been battling injustice for years through our church's programs. Why do you call this an activity for the Marketplace Minister?" Naturally, as a former pastor, I recognize this has been part of the church's agenda for years. Ministries to the poor and disenfranchised exist in almost every major metropolitan area. Still, there is a major difference when a Marketplace Minister enters this arena. He or she possesses something most ministries do not: money, influence, and authority.

As I have observed the phenomenal impact taking place in the Twin Cities, I have seen something that is rare, if not unique. Most inner-city ministries I have been acquainted with over the years have been woefully underfunded and operate with a poverty mindset. Such a tragic state of affairs causes many of these ministries to appear as impoverished as the people they seek to help.

But when an authoritative Marketplace Minister enters the battle, something interesting transpires. These people of influence call on their friends of influence. Suddenly events accelerate. This is a major reason for the rapid growth of Hope for the City. There are other organizations that are larger, but not many that have grown as quickly. As Dennis Doyle says, "My friends don't have to be Christians to give to me. They care for the poor. It's not a matter that you've got to be a Christian to give to this effort. The bottom line is: Do you want to help people?"

In the future, other Marketplace Ministers will be called upon to deal with injustice stemming from racism, poverty, discrimination, and all other forms of unfairness. I am particularly privileged to watch and participate in a movement that is discovering and equipping Marketplace Ministers in African-American communities, where the Church is growing faster than in any other segment of society.

Today this community features many of the leading pastors in America. Pastors such as Bishop T.D. Jakes, Bishop Eddie Long, Bishop Keith Butler, Bishop Shelton Bady, Bishop Noel Jones, Creflo Dollar, Bishop Earl Ray, and others are known outside their congregations and beyond their cities. Likewise, I believe that many emerging Marketplace Ministers will be people of color. Leaders like Al Hollingsworth, owner of a multimillion-dollar packaging company; and Jerome Edmondson, the first black owner of a Denny's and A&W franchises, are just two examples.

Also a speaker at marketplace ministry conferences, Hollingsworth runs Aldelano Corporation, with 1,000 employees spread over five states. His Michigan-based company produces such familiar containers as Pringles' cans and the bags holding Pop Tarts. In a recent profile, *Charisma* magazine noted that 61-year-old Hollingsworth is at the age where he could be filling his Organizer with golf appointments and lounging at resorts: "Instead, he's hard at work (in addition to running his company) teaching Christian young people and adults about the power of purpose, the benefits of hard work and how they can, just as he has, see their dreams change from vision to reality."[1]

Hollingsworth does this through a pair of educational programs he and his wife, Hattie, have designed. The one for youth ages 7 to 19 is called "Building on Spiritual Substance" (BOSS), which trains them to develop self-confidence, self-esteem, speaking abilities, and godly business skills. A parallel effort for adults, "Vertical Leap," employs biblically based, success-training seminars. The executive says these are part of the purpose God awakened in him four decades ago in college: "That's really the heartbeat of where [he and his wife] are vested. We are kingdom entrepreneurs."[2]

In his memoir, *Maximizing Misfortune: Turning Life's Failures Into Successes,* Jerome Edmondson tells of being raised by his grandmother. Although he grew up with six siblings in a two-bedroom shack in southern Missouri, he never felt the impact of poverty until he reached high school in Harmondale. There, more affluent students drove cars, wore better clothes, and paid for their own lunches while Edmondson ate free—an embarrassing fact and not easily hid.

Still, as he walked dirt roads alone, amid cotton, wheat, soybean, and milo fields, this future entrepreneur dreamed of living differently than what he saw around him. Each day the young man became more determined to become an instrument to break the curse of bondage and his family's poverty mentality: "I always had this dream of being successful. It was planted and nourished deep in my spirit in just the same way as the crops that grew up from the black earth every spring....Every year the farmer with expectations realized his dream, and I watched that farmer's field of dreams produce a harvest for him. That gave me hope that someday I could produce something within me that could provide an opportunity for my grandmother and me."[3]

Still, before eventually living his dream, Edmondson writes of how he had to overcome the failure that had been programmed into his spirit. Growing up in the country, everyone around him farmed cotton, soybeans, and corn. African-Americans formed the workforce, just as they had since the fields were first plowed. They rarely owned the land on which they labored; likewise, their expectations for the future were low. The author writes of how the best thing to do in his native area was keep your head down, stay out of trouble, and spend the weekends drinking away life's boredom.

"In order to succeed in your life you must face the failure that's been programmed into your spirit," Edmonson says. "I had to deprogram myself. You see, my identity had been tempered with the low expectations I had received. I needed to discover who I really was—not in the eyes of those around me, but in the eyes of God. Discovering my true identity was a gift—a gift that gave me the definition necessary to achieve success. Self-discovery is the first key to success, because if you don't know who you are, you will never be able to help anyone else. Identity is what opportunity demands.

"I developed faith in those fields of dreams, faith to look for something more than what I saw all around me. I grew up dreaming that I could be more and have more. I looked at that star every night and it gave me a hope that God had a vision for me. My Creator had a destiny in mind for me that offered far more than the narrow definition I had received in Harmondale."[4]

Setting Captives Free

Much of the bondage that still holds people hostage is a result of discriminatory thinking. Such misguided outlooks must be exposed and corrected. Bondage also exists because of wrong choices people made at crucial times in their lives. Some married the wrong person or got involved with drugs and dropped out of school. Many are still living with the consequences of these and other wrong choices that have led to poverty, poor job skills, and broken relationships.

Poverty represents a universal condition in the world. Likewise, a poverty mind-set afflicts people at all economic levels, not just those who grow up poor. The poverty mind-set is a stronghold of the devil. Its emphasis includes not just keeping things from people, but preventing them from fulfilling the call of God on their lives. Those who possess vast sums of money, but grapple with the fear of losing it at any moment are in this kind of bondage. Such a mind-set prods people to hoard things, whether that be money, time, or resources. The opposite, of course, is a spirit of generosity that causes people to give to God's work and help accomplish His purposes. The latter outlook needs to be an integral element of work. Those who have been given gifts need to release them so that others can walk in freedom.

The Bible says that when Adam and Eve first disobeyed God, the Lord brought a curse upon the ground. The ground was the place of provision. The business of the day was integrally connected to the soil. So when Genesis 3:17 says that God cursed the ground, its real-life application is that God cursed mankind's business and potential for provision.

However, when Jesus went to the cross, He broke the power of this curse. Many have accepted what Jesus did with regard to their personal relationship with God. However, this truth also needs to be applied to work, people's source of provision. By understanding all that Christ did, we can break the poverty mind-set. We can demolish the bondage to fear of lack of resources that fuels greed, class envy, and other conflict. Marketplace Ministers are in position to bring about this breakthrough.

As I mentioned in Chapter 2, through the years evangelists have quoted Luke 19:10 as a mandate for winning the lost. This is a fantastic verse for evangelism because we know that God does not want anyone to perish in hell. Yet it is worth noting the dramatic impact that being in the presence of Christ made on the wealthy businessman, Zacchaeus.

After Zacchaeus committed to giving half of his goods to the poor, Jesus declared that He came to offer him salvation as a child of Abraham, and then added the phrase about coming to save that which was lost. To appreciate the full impact of the Lord's words, remember all that His death on the cross accomplished. To stop short of appreciating, and living in, God's full redemptive purpose is to fall short of all that God has mandated for His children to accomplish.

When Jesus died on the cross, He became a curse for humans in order to break the curse that originated with Adam and Eve's disobedience. People no longer need to live under its power. I believe one of Marketplace Ministers' roles will be to assist the Body of Christ in coming out from under the effects of the curse. The anointing for breaking bondages fits well in the hands of workplace ministers. It incorporates a needed, previously missing dimension to the full message of the gospel. (This anointing fits with, and complements, the characteristic I will examine in Chapter 7, "Wealth Transfer.")

Millions of Christians understand that the cross became God's tool to break the curse from their lives in regard to sin—the willful and inadvertent mistakes made in life. Yet, it has a much broader meaning. Christ's power applies to every area of bondage still affecting multitudes of people. Poverty, depression, oppression, bitterness, anger, and other forms of bondage must bow when confronted with the curse-breaking power of the cross.

Paul put it best when he wrote to the Galatians, "Christ has redeemed us from the curse of the law, having become a curse for us (for it is written, 'Cursed is everyone who hangs on a tree'), that the blessing of Abraham might come upon the Gentiles in Christ Jesus, that we might receive the promise of the Spirit through faith" (Gal. 3:13-14).

God has promised "the blessing of Abraham" for His children, making this Old Testament prophet a prime example of how to live in freedom today.

Breaking Bondages

I will conclude this chapter with a brief, biblical review of bondage breaking, using Romans 8 as a guide. In verse 18 Paul talks about present suffering: "For I consider that the sufferings of this present time are not worthy to be compared with the glory which shall be revealed in us." Indeed, many today are in places of suffering or bondage. But in verse 19 (still speaking in the present tense), Paul tells of a current expectation: "For the earnest expectation of the creation eagerly waits for the revealing of the sons of God."

There are two notable truths about this verse:

1. Creation has the expectation.

2. Creation is waiting for the children of God to receive revelation.

What is this creation? The easy answer is: everything that has been created. However, a closer look reveals that Paul is speaking of something very personal. This entire chapter discusses how people can live in the freedom of the Holy Spirit. I believe that a better application of *creation* is "that which you were created for." Paul is speaking of destiny and purpose. And he is saying that this invisible, yet very real spiritual purpose (God's creation) over each life is waiting with expectation for that person to step into it.

Remember, one of God's purposes for creating mankind was for work. The center of human existence was work—in cooperation with God, and worshiping the Creator. When sin entered the world, God cursed work. In the twinkling of an eye, everything changed. Work became toil. Stress entered the picture. Labor became a burden. When Jesus died on the cross, a part of what He did was to return men and women to their original purpose, meaning work that avoided strife and bondage.

With that in mind, consider what Paul is saying in Romans 8. People's created purpose is waiting for God's revelation to dawn; as verse 20 notes, it has been subjected to futility: "For the creation was subjected to futility, not willingly, but because of Him who subjected it in hope." There are times when everyone experiences such hopelessness, working without making headway. Sales don't come through, promised raises fail to appear, the computer goes haywire, or an employee embezzles money from the business, leading it to the edge of bankruptcy.

This is what makes verse 20 so interesting, because it says that God subjected creation to futility. In other words, don't blame the devil. Yet, it also says that God had something in mind: hope. What hope? Hope that His children would figure out the power that is available to break the curse. Paul goes on to say in verse 21 that the creation (your purpose, destiny, provision/business) will be delivered from bondage into the same freedom that people walk in—"because the creation itself also will be delivered from the bondage of corruption into the glorious liberty of the children of God." In other words, the freedom received at the time of accepting Christ can be experienced at work. If someone has been delivered from an addiction to drugs, alcohol, gambling, or another habit that has held them captive for years, they can also expect God to lift bondages from their occupational life.

Someone reading this may ask, "But didn't that happen when I got saved?" I would respond that the potential and the power are there. Still, just as a person needs to personally accept Jesus (no one else can make that decision), the same principle applies. No one else can do it; people need to claim it for themselves. You can set your destiny free by declaring over your work, business, or other source of provision, "I apply the power of the blood of Jesus to you today, and break all forms of demonic bondage. I declare that you are free to provide all that God wants me to have. I shall fulfill my calling, my purpose, and my destiny."

Finally, consider verse 22, where Paul talks about the birth pangs associated with creation: "For we know that the whole creation groans and labors with birth pangs together until now." I believe that the apostle was referring to the pain that accompanies giving birth to eternal purpose. Many Christian business leaders have been serving God in their work, hoping one day to quit their job so they can "go into ministry full-time." I believe an overarching reason for today's marketplace ministry movement is so God can trumpet the message, "I called you to serve Me in your work setting. This is your purpose; this is why I gave you the gifts I did. This is what I want from you. Now step into the fullness of your destiny."

Some of you may be feeling those birth pangs as you read these words. Praise God. Today is the day for the awareness of your destiny to come forth, like a newborn babe. You can move from simply doing a job to fulfilling an eternal purpose, transformed from mere existence to godly destiny. When Dennis and Megan Doyle set out to help the poor in Minneapolis and St. Paul, they could have shut down their real estate firm and tried to do this through their church. Countless numbers of people around the world are overjoyed that they remained in their business.

Endnotes

1. "The Boss With a Big Heart," *Charisma*, February 2004, 61.

2. Ibid.

3. Jerome Edmondson, *Maximizing Fortune: Turning Life's Failures Into Success* (Shippensburg, PA: Destiny Image Publishers, 2003) 21.

4. Ibid, 45.

CHAPTER 7

Wealth Transfer

Always remember it is the Lord your God who gives you power to become rich, and He does it to fulfill the covenant He made with your ancestors (Deuteronomy 8:18 NLT).

Linda Rios Brook was on a fast track in the glamorous, influential, and lucrative profession of television management. However, en route to corporate stardom she came to a professional crossroads she had not anticipated. A simple choice transferred her from the status and recognition as the most influential woman in Minneapolis-St. Paul, Minnesota to the unemployment line.

Her choice? The CEO of the company she worked for ordered her to stop discussing her personal faith in any public setting and to stop teaching a Bible study class at her church.[1] I've heard Linda relate this story at marketplace ministry conferences; when she tells it, she makes sure that no one sees her as a martyr. She says the real choice was not the one her CEO presented, but the one the Lord Jesus gave her. She made her stand: continue publicly acknowledging Christ, which meant she had to resign from her position with a Fortune 500 company.

So how does this story fit here? Shortly after leaving her company, she and her husband, Larry, were offered an opportunity to buy a bankrupt TV station in the Twin Cities for $2.5 million. Assembling a group of 40 investors, they eventually purchased the outlet. After six years of building the station, they sold it for a profit of $50 million. That translates to a return on their investment of approximately 2,000 percent.

Thus, over a seven-year period after leaving her corporate position, Linda and her husband were led by God into a tremendous transfer of wealth that benefited His Kingdom. Many of the Christians who invested in this deal became wealthy. In the week after the sale, they signed over stock valued at approximately $2 million to Christian ministries and colleges in the Twin Cities. One local congregation received almost $800,000.[2]

In her book, *Wake Me When It's Over*, Linda tells about the lessons she learned in this venture. She tells of trying to build a television station like a church, instead of building the station as the Lord directed her to do. One interesting anecdote involved keeping her investors happy by airing well-known commentator Rush Limbaugh's TV talk show. In order to gain access to it, though, she had to air "The Jerry Springer Show"—not exactly fitting their goal to air family-friendly Christian programming. But that was the deal: To get Rush, she had to take Jerry. Linda tells how they tried to pigeonhole Springer by airing his show at 11 p.m., but still it became the station's highest rated program.[3]

Linda tells how this was used by the Lord:

Then the Lord spoke. He asked what I thought the people were like who stayed up late at night to watch programs like "The Jerry Springer Show." I thought to myself that they must be people who couldn't sleep and had nowhere to go. Maybe they were people who were looking for lives that were more desperate than their own. Maybe they were people who didn't have any friends. Then it came to me. Clear as a sterling spoon on Waterford crystal. "Need a friend? Call this number." I saw it plainly. Crawling across the bottom of the screen on "The Jerry Springer Show" at ten-minute intervals were those words.

Two of our prayer partners and faithful friends were Dan and Diane Morstad who ran a crises counseling phone center called "Love Lines." I asked Dan what he thought about putting the Love Lines phone number on the screen during The Jerry Springer Show with the "Need a friend?" message and seeing what would happen. He agreed to try it. None of us could have predicted what did happen.

From the very first night, callers overwhelmed the crises counselors....They were lost, alone, depressed, and desperate to talk to someone who might pretend to care about them. Many of them, literally *thousands* were led to the saving grace of Jesus Christ over the phone and sent for follow-up to local churches.[4]

Such an unusual outreach would likely generate bitter criticism in conventional church circles, but God is in the people-saving business no matter how strange the approach seems on the surface. Likewise, God wants to use your business to help build His Kingdom. As shown by Linda Rios Brook's story, He also wants to bless you financially as you serve Him in this kind of ministry.

As amazing as this story is, I have seen or heard of similar scenarios in Germany, Israel, England, the Philippines, Canada, throughout the Caribbean, and across the United States. About the time I began writing this book, I spoke at a large church in northern California. I had been there a year earlier. The first morning two couples came up to me with the same message: "You prayed for us a year ago and we started our own business." One couple was running a popular ice cream franchise. The other had started an investment firm.

Both got involved in these endeavors after several people prayed for them and they responded to God's direction. Acting on the ideas He gave them, they are living out the reality of His leading and reaping the rewards—not just financially, but of rich relationships and doing their part to make their communities better, more prosperous places to live.

Creating Wealth

God has no plan for the transfer of wealth except business. Sound radical? Anti-scriptural? Unrealistic? If you accept the traditional interpretations of the Bible that have been preached for centuries, this statement may even upset you. However, that is because too many Christians have failed to look at the Bible through the eyes of a businessperson. This topic is so crucial that it deserves some additional, biblically based instruction.

God works in mysterious ways. For instance, one evening Wilma and I were having dinner with our good friends, Paul and Donna Cox, when Paul told me that God had given him a message to deliver. Over the years, I have received a number of these types of prophetic words. Some have lasted for 15 or 20 minutes. I have often typed up these lengthy messages and studied them to comprehend their full dimension and application to my life. Others have been much shorter, such as a paragraph or just a sentence. This particular one was even more brief.

"The Lord has told me that this word is the third important piece, or phase, or element, of your ministry," Paul said. "Number one being that ministry is to happen in the workplace, out in the marketplace, not just in the church. Number two, that revival will come out there (meaning at work), not necessarily in here (the church). It could happen just as easily at the job as here. The third phase will come out of this word."

By now, I was all ears.

"Here's the word: 'Midian.' "

"Can you tell me a little bit more, please?" I asked.

"No, that's it. Just Midian."

"Well, what's it mean?"

"It's your word, not mine. Go figure it out."

Although I knew who Midian was, I had forgotten about the significance of this Old Testament character. So, though a bit perplexed, I started studying Midian in the Bible and discovered some interesting truths.

As a refresher course for those who aren't up on Bible trivia, Midian was one of the sons of Abraham. Most people never get beyond Abraham and Sarah's two famous sons: Ishmael and Isaac. However, soon after Isaac married Rebekah, Sarah died. Abraham married for a second time. His next wife, Keturah, bore him six more sons, including Midian. This son became the head of the tribe that would be known as the Midianites. They show up periodically throughout the Old Testament.

Continuing my study, I saw that Midian's ancestors became traders and merchants. They were businesspeople involved in the multinational industries of their time. Ironically, it was a band of Midianites who purchased Joseph from his brothers and then sold him in Egypt (see Gen. 37:28). Midianites also seduced the children of Israel (see Num. 25) and fought against Gideon (see Judg. 6). This may lead some to say, "So why are you excited about them? They're on the wrong side of God."

Usually, they were. Still, consider the first instance listed above. Because of them, Joseph reached Egypt, which represented his destiny. God used the battle Gideon faced to teach this prophet how to trust in Him instead of his large army. Then there was the key lesson that Moses learned from Jethro, his father-in-law, while leading the children of Israel into the Promised Land. Jethro was a businessman. Pastors like to mention that he was the priest of Midian, but they overlook the fact that prior to this, Moses was out tending Jethro's flock of sheep. As a businessman, Jethro hired someone to care for his assets.

To paraphrase the story from Exodus 18, after Moses took Israel out of Egypt, he was preparing to lead the nation into their freedom when Jethro asked, "Are you going to organize them?"

"I don't know how," Moses replied.

Since Jethro understood management, administration, and other details needed to manage a large corporation, he spelled out a plan: select capable leaders from among the people, divided into rulers of thousands, hundreds, fifties, and tens. Then let these leaders judge disputes and other matters among the people. If there is something too weighty or complex, they can bring it to Moses, but otherwise let these leaders oversee the tribes' business.

"So it will be easier for you, for they will bear the burden with you," Jethro promised. "If you do this thing, and God so commands you, then you will be able to endure, and all this people will also go to their place in peace" (Ex. 18:22b-23).

So, not only were the Midianites used of God in more than one way, but as I researched this topic further, I saw that they were involved in the wealth transfer that the Lord had promised would come to His children.

A key passage to understanding this truth appears in Isaiah 60:5-6: "Then you shall see and become radiant, and your heart shall swell with joy; because the abundance of the sea shall be turned to you, the wealth of the Gentiles shall come to you. The multitude of camels shall cover your land, the dromedaries of Midian and Ephah; all those from Sheba shall come; they shall bring gold and incense, and they shall proclaim the praises of the Lord."

Did you catch the significance? It says the wealth of the Gentiles (unbelievers) is coming to God's children on the camels of Midian. This is a clue to what God wants to do. For years, people have operated on the promise of "give and it shall be given unto you." While that is true, it leaves out a necessary piece of the puzzle: business. This is what we see through Midian—namely, the reality that God wants to bless your business. He wants to bless your work.

Miracle Mentality

Many Christians have heard some kind of teaching about the coming transfers of wealth. Church members love the promises of God with regard to this, such as:

- Proverbs 13:22b, which says, "The wealth of the sinner is stored up for the righteous."

- We love to claim our part in the inheritance that will come through Abraham: "And in you all the families of the earth shall be blessed" (Gen. 12:3b).

- The one I discovered in my study of Midian: "The wealth of the Gentiles shall come to you," found in Isaiah 60:5b. This promise is repeated in verse 11b: "That men may bring to you the wealth of the Gentiles...."

These verses can excite any crowd. Indeed, I have heard others use them to stir people up before taking an offering. The speaker will build the momentum and come to the conclusion that when you give to this offering, you can get ready for the wealth transfer that God has promised. A number of other verses are frequently used to emphasize this point. These include Scriptures about giving so that God can give back to you, sowing and reaping, or a mention of a thirty, sixty, or hundredfold return.

Now all these verses are true; they are Bible promises. However, most of us have yet to see the wealth transfer. It is still a future dream. So we hold onto those promises with the expectation that any day God might fulfill His Word. When that happens, our bank accounts will be miraculously and supernaturally filled (or at least we cling to a faint hope that it will happen).

The problem is that this outlook leads to what I referred to in Chapter 2—adopting a miracle-based mentality. I believe in miracles and thank God for them. The church I grew up in taught they no longer existed. However, my outlook changed after our daughter, and then our son, were healed supernaturally. Although we didn't believe in miracles, our children's healings showed us that God still does.

As much as I love miracles, there is something better—namely, not needing a miracle. If you have cancer, you need a miraculous healing, but better not to have cancer in the first place. If you're a million dollars in debt, you will need a miracle to claw your way to solvency. Even better is to have a million dollars in the bank. All of us should want to reach the place where we don't have to rely on miracles. Far better to operate in the superabundant flow of God's resources—and that process is business.

Granted, it may not be quite as exciting as walking out to your mailbox, finding the latest Reader's Digest Sweepstakes entry, and exclaiming, "Oh, praise God. I know this is my winning number because I put a check in the offering yesterday and God promised a return. I know this time I'm going to win." Or rationalizing playing the lottery with the statement, "Okay, I gave $1,000 to the church, now I'll go buy 100 tickets." But God's plan to supply your needs isn't the lottery, the Reader's Digest Sweepstakes, or Publisher's Clearinghouse; neither is the church or government. God's system for wealth transfer is business.

After Isaiah 60:5-6 talks about Midian's camels carrying gold to God's children, verse 9 adds, "Surely the coastlands shall wait for Me; and the ships of Tarshish will come first, to bring your sons from afar, their silver and their gold with them." I have studied the ships of Tarshish. They were the modern-day equivalent of a multinational corporation. Whether the delivery comes by Federal Express, UPS, email, wire transfer, job, or business, God says He will bring gold to His children. But it is integrally connected to Midian and the ships of Tarshish, which had business at their core.

God Blesses Work

If you doubt this thesis, look at Deuteronomy 14:28-29, which is part of a lengthy discourse by Moses to the children of Israel. Over several chapters, he spells out various laws and practices God has told them to follow. In this particular verse, Moses tells the Israelites that they are to bring a tithe (ten percent) of their produce every third year to help supply the needs of the Levites—their priests. The clincher appears at the end of verse 29: "That the Lord your God may bless you in all the work of your hand which you do."

When you give, you open the door to blessings, but usually not through an immediate miracle. Instead, it is the Lord's blessing on the work of your hands. This message is reiterated in the next chapter, where Moses talks about giving to the poor and needy. Deuteronomy 15:10 says, "You shall surely give to him, and your heart should not be grieved when you give to him, because for this thing the Lord your God will bless you in *all your works and in all to which you put your hand*" (emphasis added).

A similar message appears in Deuteronomy 16:15, "Seven days you shall keep a sacred feast to the Lord your God in the place which the Lord chooses, because the Lord your God will *bless you in all your produce and in all the work of your hands,* so that you surely rejoice" (emphasis added).

Although long ignored, the point of these Scriptures is that God wants us to connect the dots. Instead of praying for a miraculous windfall when you give, give and connect your work with provision. When you give, God opens blessings on your labors. Instead of despising your job, griping about how hard you're working without getting anywhere, moaning about the lack of recognition you're receiving, or hatching a scheme to quit; try following the Lord's plan. God is literally telling you, "Follow My principles and let Me add My blessing to your work."

Now, giving is not the only connector. Another is to pray in faith, believing that God will give you work to do with your hands that will return to you the blessing that God has promised. When that comes, it can represent a steady flow of provision. Instead of hoping an unexpected check shows up in the mail, you can expect God to deliver week after week, month after month, year after year. Because you are faithful in prayer, apply your ability to hear God's voice, and translate His guidance into the workplace; you can look for new ideas and blessings. This may not happen tomorrow, but you can trust that it will occur in God's timing.

After all, what happens if you get excited about a miracle taking place tomorrow, but it doesn't come? You may easily lose your joy, not to mention your faith. The goal is to reach the place where you can trust God to provide every single day because your life is attuned to Him. This goes back to Isaiah 60:11, where it says, "Therefore your gates shall be open continually; they shall not be shut day or night, that men may bring to you the wealth of the Gentiles."

I have seen this truth operate. At one meeting where I spoke, a man talked about a number of family members accepting Christ, as well as a friend who is a scientist. He also talked about having an abundance of money. When I asked where it came from, he replied, "It comes through the normal flow of work. And, since I have an abundance of money, I'm counseling others on how to use it."

The Marketplace Minister's Role

Marketplace Ministers were made for such a time as this. The God-given plan for wealth production and transfer is business. The government cannot produce wealth. Its primary function is to take it. Certainly the church is not a wealth-producing machine; it has other responsibilities. Knowing that God has promised wealth transfers, promised to bless the work of our hands, and called some to serve Him in the workplace, we can understand how God plans for wealth to come into His Kingdom. He is training a group of workplace ministers to create great wealth. It is one of the seven primary signs of such leaders.

I believe that the Lord has a specific plan for Marketplace Ministers in the business arena. There are untapped resources, creative ideas, and new business ventures that are just waiting to be launched. It is up to workplace ministers to learn how to hear the voice of God, tap into His stream of information, and operate with the power of the Holy Spirit. For some, this will come via current ventures, such as more efficient processes, God-directed management, and marketing and sales innovations. For others, there are new discoveries, inventions, and business plans that have remained hidden—until now.

I am confident that some of these ideas are in Scripture and that diligent study will bring them forth. As an example, a friend in England is nearing a breakthrough as he seeks to reveal information about uncovering ancient trade routes. He is looking for and finding answers in the Books of Jeremiah and Proverbs. Others will come through divine revelation, but whatever the means, God is the source.

For years Christians have heard prophetic messages about the transfer of wealth. The Bible speaks of this, as I referenced earlier, but now we are beginning to see this occur. In January 2004, news broke about the largest bequest ever given to a Christian organization. In her will, the late Joan Kroc—wife of the founder of the McDonald's hamburger chain—included a $1.5 billion-dollar gift to the Salvation Army to help them establish community centers. Thus, money generated from business endeavors will move into God's work.

Soon after that, Peter Wagner told me about a gift from the Geneva Fund in Switzerland to help rebuild the African nation of Ivory Coast. This grant, equivalent to $1 billion in U.S. dollars, is earmarked for building six hospitals, a university, a seminary, 20,000 houses, orphanages, teaching bases, and agricultural centers. Significantly, pastor Dion Robert, leader of one of the nation's largest churches, will oversee the administration of these funds.

Hopefully, such astonishing developments will help build Christians' faith and belief that God will provide additional resources. I am not talking about building your faith to receive a gift so you can spend it on yourself (see Jas. 4:3). Instead, I pray that you develop the faith that you can become the kind of wise leader who builds a business prosperous enough to make such generous donations.

Endnotes

1. Linda Rios Brook, *Wake Me When It's Over* (Baltimore, MD: America House Book Publishers, 2001) 34.

2. Ibid, 166.

3. Ibid, 140.
4. Ibid, 148-149.

CHAPTER 8

Hearing the Voice of God

Today you must listen to His voice. Don't harden your hearts against Him (Hebrews 3:7-8 NLT).

A few months ago, Julian Watts—the English businessman I mentioned in Chapter 2—called me to arrange a meeting during a visit to the United States. Sensing God leading him to line up prayer intercessors across the U.S. before introducing his product here, he wanted to present his new Internet-based business venture to me. We arranged to meet at a hotel in Southern California. I came expecting to have a cup of coffee and casually discuss his venture. However, to my surprise, when I arrived, Julian led me into a conference room with two projectors set up and a full table of materials on display. When I asked who else would be at the meeting, he said, "Just the three of us." That meant Julian, who is the chief executive officer; his firm's president, and me.

Next, Julian unrolled an impressive, professionally-prepared presentation, with a finely-tuned script displayed in printed handouts and on PowerPoint slides. Unfortunately, the material quickly left me feeling like I was foraging through a strange jungle with no compass. Since the technology rose above my level of comprehension, I was feeling uncertain of how to respond afterward. In the middle of his presentation, I said quietly, "Lord, speak to me. I know these men want my input, but I am not sure what to say."

As soon as I prayed, the Lord showed me a picture. When I receive pictures from the Lord, they can move rapidly from scene to scene without much seeming connection.

In the first picture I saw the CEO driving a race car. Though traveling at lightning speed, he zoomed around the track in the wrong direction. Next, he stopped, stepped out of his car, and walked up the stadium steps to the press box, where a 747 airplane waited for him. When I saw the airplane, the Lord showed me it was like coal barges leaving Newcastle, Australia—a place I had visited. (Newcastle is the world's second largest coal producing region.) These barges were carrying the cargo at supersonic speeds. Finally, I saw the airplane landing in a desert-like place as three people approached. I sensed that the Lord would use this shipment of goods to bring peace there.

At the end of the presentation, Julian asked me for my input. I replied, "First, let me tell about a picture that the Lord gave me during the presentation." As soon as I added, "I saw you driving a race car, but you were going the wrong direction around the track," Julian broke into tears. As I went on and related how God had shown me the 747 jet representing the coal barges from Newcastle, the president also started to weep. Here were two men from London whom I had never met in person, yet the Lord had something to say to them.

Julian told me that at one time he had been a professional race car driver. One of the tests for licensing was to navigate the track at a certain speed, but in the wrong direction. When I told him what I had seen, he could hear the Holy Spirit whispering, "Julian, you have passed the test." Much to my surprise, the president of the London-based company was from Newcastle, Australia. My vision of coal barges there was a sign from the Lord that he was in the right place. And, the 747 airplane landing in the desert confirmed a vision God had given these men earlier about using their business as a means to bring peace and transformation in the Middle East. Going into the meeting, I knew none of that—just what God showed me.

These men did not need my input about a presentation I didn't fully comprehend, but they did need to hear from God. The Lord put us together in that hotel conference room so that He could speak a word to them about their future business direction. God is like that. After we have planned, sweated, dreamed, outlined, polished our presentations, and given that legendary "110 percent," then He steps in with an authoritative word that makes the difference.

A Slight Edge

I once heard a business consultant deliver a prescription for success. His presentation featured the idea that those who succeed in business work slightly harder than anyone else. Spending a little more time at the office, making one more phone call, or getting up a few minutes earlier in the morning—those little things symbolize their small measure of extra effort. The consultant termed this the "Principle of the Slight Edge." Despite a well-crafted message, he missed the point. The idea of fashioning a principle on hard work is a popular idea, particularly in America where busting one's gut is esteemed as part of the necessary drive to amass wealth. However, this is not a God idea. God wants to give us the edge without turning us into workaholics.

As we study the Bible and discover more about God's intentions, we learn that He created us for work. It is an inherent part of our nature and part of the Genesis purpose of creation. But the kind of grueling, stress-inducing toil that afflict many in modern times is a result of human disobedience to God and the resulting curse that He placed on work. This means hard work is not the "slight edge" for which so many are searching.

By contrast, the authentic "Principle of the Slight Edge" is found in spiritual realms. It is the ability to hear the voice of God for your business. Businesspersons around the globe are searching for a competitive edge—a crucial idea that moves them ahead of the pack, a perfectly timed product launch, the right connection, or just plain luck. Occasionally, it appears as if one of them has found the secret formula. However, most of these seekers are looking in all the wrong places.

God wants to give His children an edge, not so they can whip the competition, but in order to bless the community and move His Kingdom forward. The Lord is speaking today more clearly than most of us have ever experienced. Businessmen and women attuned to God's Spirit are listening for, and hearing, God's voice. They are finding that He is not only interested in their work, but He wants to bless and prosper it. The Lord wants their business to become the factor that makes a vital difference in their communities, nations, and the world.

I base this claim on personal observation. I have seen the word of the Lord come at the right moment to save businesses from disaster or ultimate ruin. I have watched as God snatched a company from the brink of bankruptcy with a clear word and direction for the future. I have seen the frustrated become the anointed and discouraged leaders revitalized into successful CEOs. If you want to get the edge at work, you must develop your skills in hearing from God. He is speaking today and has directions to give if you will learn to listen.

The Lord will give you keen insights that allow you to look into the future of business and see what is coming and what is needed. This kind of hearing is not available to the natural ear, but it is there for the workplace minister who will learn to tune his or her ear to the Lord's ever-present voice. God's Kingdom is advancing as never before. I pray that you will be a part of the great army that the Lord is raising up—the army with the slight edge!

Business Interpretations

As I mentioned in Chapter 2, Richard and Pauline Fleming, Marketplace Ministers in England, have developed what they call

Kingdom Advice Centres. These are training outposts designed to help business leaders and employees hear God's voice in the marketplace. In recent years, as I have worked alongside businessmen and women, I have found that most workplace ministries are lacking the key ingredient that has the potential to thrust them over the top—namely, teaching (and the resulting practice) about hearing the voice of God.

It helps to realize that:

- God is concerned about your daily life;
- He cares about your work; and
- He will speak with you about it.

When you discover these truths, it will transform your work life. Those in the marketplace need to learn the practice of hearing God's voice. Hearing from God is one of the foundations for serving Him in a marketplace setting. One of God's mandates for us is equipping others for the work of ministry. Therefore, it is essential that those who have learned how to hear from God teach and train others in this art.

Although I served for years as a pastor, businessman Richard Fleming has been one of my role models in learning more about this skill, particularly in the context of the workplace. Thanks to his influence, a couple years ago we started a Kingdom Advice Center (American spelling) in San Jose, California, with others being implemented in various cities across the U.S.

As I mentioned earlier, in the past, conventional interpretations typically directed everyone who was called into God's service into a church-type role. Rarely did anyone relate a calling to ministry with fulfilling that call in business. At Kingdom Advice Centers, our guidelines dictate not prophesying anybody away from their workplace and into a church setting. (Not that this can never happen, but we want participants oriented to fulfilling God's calling in their vocation.) Our focus is on work settings; we need to hear from God about work. When it comes to your occupation,

God will never run out of good ideas. As you give to Him, in return He will speak to you and give you ideas about your work.

Lately, I have been studying Jeremiah 6:16, where it says, "Thus says the Lord: 'Stand in the ways and see, and ask for the old paths, where the good way is, and walk in it; then you will find rest for your souls....' " I have read every commentary I can put my hands on about this passage. Most scholars say it means that you're walking down a road; there will be a fork in it; and you have to make sure whether to turn right or left.

However, I think this also can refer to an ancient business path. Literally, I think this refers to a trade route that will lead to prosperity. This is the message I have been hearing through my Bible studies and prayer. I believe that if you can get on that silk road that runs from China and find out what God is blessing, it will yield riches untold. The least of these is money. More important are influence, peace, and stability.

One day as I was praying about this and other prophetic words I have heard, I sensed the Holy Spirit whispering, "Queen Esther's beauty products." I chuckled, "Lord, that can't be for me. I don't know anything about beauty products. If I did, I wouldn't know what to do with them." However, since that is what God told me, I believe those products lie somewhere on that ancient path. Someone reading this book will probably figure it out and become a millionaire.

Hearing, Not Prophecy

I know a number of people who operate in the gift of prophecy. This is a wonderful gift, one that greatly benefits the Body of Christ. I have personally received direction for my life and ministry through prophetic messages. I thank God for the prophets who are active in the world, including those who operate in the marketplace. We need them and long for their input. However, my emphasis in this chapter is not on prophecy, but the ability to hear God's voice.

The apostle Paul is a perfect example of a Marketplace Minister who heard from God. A builder, a tent maker, and a man who earned a living working with his hands, Paul wrote nearly half the New Testament. He is viewed as the greatest example of an apostle in the Church age. Paul was also a strategic thinker; it is obvious that he received his strategies through close communication with the Lord. As you read his writings, you cannot help but realize that everything he did helped promote the gospel of Jesus.

When Paul defended his apostleship in First Corinthians 9, he made it known that God's plan includes financial support for ministers who preach the gospel: "...For our sakes, no doubt, this is written, that he who plows should plow in hope, and he who threshes in hope should be partaker of his hope. If we have sown spiritual things for you, is it a great thing if we reap your material things?...Even so the Lord has commanded that those who preach the gospel should live from the gospel" (verses 10-11,14).

However, Paul also made it clear that he would not be among the paid clergy. In verse 15 he writes, "But I have used none of these things, nor have I written these things that it should be done so to me; for it would be better for me to die than that anyone should make my boasting void." In other words, Paul established his apostleship as a worker in the marketplace.

As I read about Paul's life, it appears that he worked a full Monday-through-Friday shift. Then, on the weekend he went to the synagogue to preach. Did he minister during the week? Undoubtedly, he did on the job. But that which the church has focused on—his preaching and missionary service—represented more of a weekend endeavor. This is spelled out in Acts 18:3-4, "So, because he was of the same trade, he stayed with them and worked; for by occupation they were tentmakers. And he reasoned in the synagogue every Sabbath, and persuaded both Jews and Greeks."

Paul had a plan, which went far beyond his ability to produce more tents than his cohorts (not that he didn't use his business). Acts 18 also contains an account of Paul meeting Aquila. The Bible says that Paul moved into the home of Aquila and his wife, Priscilla, because they worked in the same occupation. Yet it includes the note that Paul "found him." I believe this was part of the apostle's strategy. He used his skill in business to gain contacts, both for business and ministry.

The workplace minister will have a strategy for both arenas. And the truth is we need the kind of strategic thinking used by Marketplace Ministers. Many pastors today have their roots in workplace settings and operate much like CEOs of major corporations. Still, most pastors are shepherds, who do not naturally think in strategic terms. This isn't a negative, because we also need people who think in shepherding terms. We need pastors who care for their flocks by feeding and protecting them.

As much as I thank God for pastors, though, I am thankful for strategic thinkers in the workplace. Those who are able to think strategically can hear from God, look into the future, and determine what God plans for the future.

God Speaks

For some practical examples, consider the lesson illustrated in Numbers chapter 12. Aaron and Miriam, the brother and sister of Moses, were mumbling and complaining. In addition to complaining about Moses' wife, they were grumbling about the fact that it seemed as if no one knew that they, too, could hear from God. As they talked about it, God heard them (see v. 2). Talk about a shock!

The Bible says not only did God hear, He summoned them to a meeting. After the Lord had reminded them of the humility of Moses, He said, "Hear now My words: If there is a prophet among you, I, the Lord, make Myself known to him in a vision; I speak to him in a dream. Not so with My servant Moses; he is faithful in all My house. I speak with him face to face, even plainly, and not in dark sayings; and he sees the form of the Lord. Why then were you not afraid to speak against My servant Moses?" (vs. 6-8)

In this passage, God relates four ways that He can—and does—speak to His children:

1. Visions.

2. Dreams.

3. Face-to-face.

4. Dark sayings.

We can expect the Lord to speak to us in these same ways today. I will narrow them down to three general ways that the Lord may speak to us: pictures, words, or spontaneous thoughts.

Pictures

The difference between dreams and visions is whether you are awake or asleep. While you are sleeping God can give dreams (pictures), and while you are awake He can take you into a vision (pictures). In both cases the Lord is giving a message in the form of a picture. I have experienced both of these in powerful ways. There have been times that I have asked for a dream, and the Lord has provided a clear answer and direction for my situation.

However, you do not need to go to sleep in order for the Lord to speak to you. You can enter into a time of prayer right at your desk and ask the Lord for a word, a picture, or a thought from Him. I have discovered that many people "see" the pictures more quickly than they "hear" the words. The picture at first may not make a lot of sense, but as you seek the Lord for its meaning, it usually becomes clear.

Words

Like Moses, some hear more directly at times as if the Lord is speaking to them face-to-face. Some will even testify to hearing the audible voice of God. However, I have found this to be less common. Usually when someone says that he hears the voice of God, he is referring to words that form in his mind. Often, the message is as distinct as audible words; people are even able to carry on a conversation with the Lord. Rather than being actual spoken words, though, these are thoughts that come into the mind in a time of worship and prayer, or while seeking to hear from the Lord. There have been times in my life that I knew the Lord was speaking to me, which is consistent with the teaching in John 10 about His sheep knowing His voice.

Spontaneous Thoughts

Another way the Lord speaks to us is through what are termed "dark sayings." These are more like riddles, or words and thoughts that at first we do not fully understand. Initially, they may not make sense. Often someone cannot quite verbalize what the Lord is telling him or her, so they simply say, "It feels right" or "It doesn't feel right." However, as we continue through our circumstances and continue to pray, we come to understand the meaning of the Lord's words.

When businesspersons and pastors gather together at Kingdom Advice Centers, we ask the Lord to speak to us in these three ways: pictures, words, and thoughts (or senses). In these settings we pray more in line with the way one would do at work. In a church setting, there may be a worship leader, a praise band, and a time of worship, with specific songs on the agenda. In the workplace, we cannot call in the worship leader and the band; we must learn to worship without those aids.

I love to worship with a group when both the leader and the band are anointed; those can be special times. However, in a workplace setting, the worship is much different. In the Kingdom Advice Center, when we worship, some will pray out loud and others will pray silently. Some will sing and others will walk the floor. Some might kneel in prayer while others lean on the wall; some might even beat on the wall.

In such times of spontaneous worship, we ask the Lord to speak to us.

And He does.

We will then record what we have heard, seen, or sensed from the Lord. Since I like to record these words and pictures, we will often use a large erasable board or poster-sized Post-it Notes.

At a recent gathering, some saw pictures of tall buildings. Others had visions of green pastures or flowing waters, all with bright light shining on them. All these pictures were related to real estate and were consistent with the terrain around the city. As people related what they were seeing, we heard words about building and tools. Some felt the meeting would have significant impact in their area. Along that line, the previous night I had a dream about a real estate firm named "Diamond Real Estate." It was so specific I thought someone at the meeting would work for that company or be thinking of starting a business with that name. But no one responded when I described my dream.

Near the end of the meeting, though, a man had an interpretation of the dream. He said it was not a company; but that the dream represented the entire group and that God wanted His people to take the area (real estate) for Him. He saw the diamond as the reflector of light that God was shining that night as He called His children to take possession of the land for His Kingdom.

So, in that setting, we experienced dreams, visions, words, and thoughts from the Lord that formed a basis for transformation of the area. I'm looking forward to seeing what develops in the months and years ahead. Need a similar divine vision for your life? This is what God wants to do for you, not only for your business, but for your future. He will speak, but only if you will listen.

CHAPTER 9

Biblical Entrepreneurs

So he called ten of his servants, delivered to them ten minas, and said to them, "Do business till I come" (Luke 19:13).

Riverview Community Bank in the Elk River, Minnesota, area opened its doors in March 2003, backed by $5.5 million of investment capital. Prior to opening, the founders met with federal bank officials and projected reaching $16 million in deposits by their first anniversary, a healthy growth rate. They also forecasted writing 15 to 20 loans a month from their mortgage division, which in atypical fashion started operations two weeks prior to the opening of the bank.

A year later, bank examiners' eyes popped when deposits reached $50 million, with 85 percent of those funds lent in the community. New mortgages have ranged from 30 to 50 per month, depending on prevailing interest rates and other conditions. Not only did that rank Riverview (located in a small community—Elk River has fewer than 20,000 people) alongside larger banks in wealthy suburban areas, but this growth came amid competition from two locally-owned, century-old banks and a host of nationally networked banks and mortgage lenders.

Equally impressive is the spiritual activity occurring at Riverview. In its first 52 weeks of business, senior vice president Chuck Ripka recorded 53 people praying to receive Jesus Christ as Savior and Lord, including a Hindu. More than 40 people were healed, including one out-of-town visitor who came by with a pastor one evening so Ripka could pray for him. Soon after, the man learned his prostate cancer had vanished. Chuck commonly prays with people (including non-customers) in the conference room, his office, or over the phone.

When the bank started, Chuck told the head teller, Gloria, "The Lord has shown me you are going to be praying with customers at the drive-thru. I take the authority that I have as the senior vice president and give you permission and release you to do that which the Lord leads you to do." About six months later, Gloria noticed that a customer was struggling, and offered to pray for her. The following week the woman returned and came inside the bank to thank Gloria for praying for her that day.

A few days after Gloria first prayed for that woman, she noticed another customer struggling and asked if she could pray for him. When he agreed, she asked if he wanted to come in or remain at the drive-thru. "The drive-thru is fine," replied the man, who responded positively to the offer. Gloria continues to watch for other opportunities.

Although Ripka had been in charge of the mortgage division, early in 2004 his partner, Duane Kropuenske, shifted Chuck to business development. Duane told Chuck his ministry and evangelism were as valuable as his innate business expertise. So, Duane recreated Chuck's position to relieve him of some of his supervisory duties. He wanted to give Chuck more flexibility that would provide additional time to continue his ministry activities.

Now involved in commercial lending, Ripka says he doesn't have to do much prospecting for customers: "I have so many people wanting to do business with me that I just have to answer the phone and run through information with them. Then I sit down with our commercial lender and make sure these loans line up with what we need them to do."

Chuck's mortgage banking experience goes back to 1990, but his spiritual walk started in 1980 when he decided to follow Christ. Two years later God directed him and his wife, Kathi, to pray for his mother, a chronic alcoholic. She was lying in a hospital, unconscious. Ripka replied, "Okay, Lord, but it's one o'clock in the morning. If this is You, I need to see her come out of her coma and say yes to You." When he got to her room, he asked her to wake up. She opened her eyes and nodded in agreement to his prayer acknowledging Christ as Savior and Lord. A few days later, she died.

After he left her room, the Lord spoke to him and said, "Because of your obedience I will give you the rest of your family." Eventually, his father, brothers, sisters, and all five of his children made the same decision to follow Christ. Another major event occurred during a 40-day fast prior to his 40th birthday in 1999. During that six-week period he saw God's hand coming down out of Heaven, holding three gold keys. When Chuck asked what this meant, the Lord said, "They represent the marketplace, government, and church. I'm going to give you favor in all three arenas."

Prayer in the Marketplace

Since then, Chuck has led prayer walks through the schools in his community (located 35 miles north of Minneapolis) and in the state capitol. A participant in a weekly prayer meeting of pastors and businesspersons, he once invited the mayor, police chief, sheriff, superintendent of schools, and other local and state officials to the meeting. All agreed to come and share prayer needs with the group.

Among them was a request from the police chief concerning a raging problem with methamphetamine labs. In addition, he wanted prayer concerning four juvenile delinquents who were wreaking havoc in the city. Within two weeks of the group's prayers came the largest drug bust in Elk River's history. A month later, the four teenagers were arrested in a neighboring county and sent to a juvenile detention center.

In September 2000, the year after receiving his vision, Chuck told the audience at a mayor's prayer breakfast that a $108 million school referendum would pass. Earmarked for construction of a new building and additional personnel and instructional supplies, this measure had already been twice rejected by voters in two consecutive years. Despite a prediction by the city's newspaper that it would fail again, the referendum passed by an overwhelming margin. Recently, when a new superintendent needed additional funding for expansion in the fast-growing area, he called Ripka to ask him to pray for that referendum.

Not surprisingly, employees get considerable spiritual guidance from the bank officer, who each day prays with two or three employees, customers, or other visitors. Ripka feels comfortable in that role, since a few days before the bank opened he sensed God bringing him a message.

" 'I want you to pastor the bank,' " Chuck says the Lord told him. " 'Everything I've taught you, I want you to teach them.' So I've been teaching the staff how to pray with customers, watch for opportunities to bless people, and get them out of their comfort zone. I tell them to watch for opportunities to reach out to people. Some of our employees put Christian artwork in their offices. One said, 'We're not as bold as you, but if anyone says anything about our art we take it as a sign we can talk about God.' "

Do you see a difference between the way Chuck Ripka does business and the way your employer operates? Or, if you are the owner, in the way you conduct your business? In the days ahead, I believe we will be able to point to more stories such as this one. The excitement in that community has even generated a book: *The Elk River Story: Transforming the Spiritual Climate of a City*, which was compiled by Rick Heeren, an associate of evangelist Ed Silvoso. It mentions how this effort to break down denominational barriers and extend a witness into the marketplace has spread to two other areas of Minnesota and two cities in Wisconsin.

True biblical entrepreneurs will always have two stories to tell. One will be about seeing the blessing of God on the business— knowing the peace of His presence and the energizing of His power. The second story will relate the blessing of God in terms of financial increase. When only one of these realms is emphasized, business owners get into trouble. I have known people who have used their business as a platform for ministry activities, such as outreach, evangelism, and mercy. Yet in that process, they lost most of their profit base. One reason is they tried to imitate the nuclear church to the point that they lost sight of their business's profit-making purpose. On the other hand, I have seen others so focused on money they never found time for mercy, prayer, or practical expressions of their Christianity.

Considering Riverview Community Bank's success, biblical entrepreneurs must recognize this truth: Profit is not a dirty word. They must remember there are two reasons for their business: 1) to provide secure employment and promote peace and stability; 2) to offer customers, suppliers, and competitors a way to discover eternal truth. If in the midst of spiritual activity, your business isn't showing a profit, something is wrong. Certainly, any business must generate profits to survive, expand, and withstand the downturns in natural economic cycles. The fact that God wants to use businesses to bless the community does not negate the call to establish a profit-based business.

Parable of the Talents

Not everyone is going to run a business, whether for reasons of time, financial resources, inclinations, or personality. Besides, once entrepreneurs start a business, they will eventually need vice presidents, managers, clerks, and assorted aides to help carry out their plans. So, it is worth discussing the other side of the coin when it comes to living as a follower of Christ in the marketplace.

To gain some perspective in a world where class envy and conflict have made *success* and *prosperity* synonymous with *exploitation*, look at Christ's teaching. In Luke's Gospel, Jesus tells the story of the conversion of Zacchaeus, whose practices had made him wealthy. Jesus was addressing Zacchaeus when He said, "Today salvation has come to this house...for the Son of Man has come to seek and to save that which was lost" (Lk. 19:9-10).

In Chapter 2, I pointed out that we have misinterpreted that verse to refer only to lost people, when Jesus wanted to point His children to the broader aspect of all that was lost when Adam and Eve disobeyed God. That which was lost includes the proper treatment of our work life as well. In this context Jesus tells the following parable:

> *Therefore He said: "A certain nobleman went into a far country to receive for himself a kingdom and to return. So he called ten of his servants, delivered to them ten minas, and said to them, "Do business till I come." But his citizens hated him, and sent a delegation after him, saying, "We will not have this man to reign over us." And so it was that when he returned, having received the kingdom, he then commanded these servants, to whom he had given the money, to be called to him, that he might know how much every man had gained by trading. Then came the first, saying, "Master, your mina has earned ten minas." And he said to him, "Well done, good servant; because you were faithful in a very little, have authority over ten cities." And the second came, saying, "Master, your mina has earned five minas." Likewise he said to him, "You also be over five cities." Then another came, saying, "Master, here is your mina, which I have kept put away in a handkerchief. For I feared you, because you are an austere man. You collect what you did not deposit, and reap what you did not sow."*
>
> *And he said to him, "Out of your own mouth I will judge you, you wicked servant. You knew that I was an austere man, collecting what I did not deposit and reaping what I did not sow.*

Why then did you not put my money in the bank, that at my coming I might have collected it with interest?" And he said to those who stood by, "Take the mina from him, and give it to him who has ten minas." (But they said to him, "Master, he has ten minas.") "For I say to you, that to everyone who has will be given; and from him who does not have, even what he has will be taken away from him. But bring here those enemies of mine, who did not want me to reign over them, and slay them before me" (Luke 19:12-27).

To translate this parable into a modern-day, corporate scenario, imagine a CEO of a multinational corporation based in the United States. This executive faces an opportunity to expand his business by using his influence and net worth to take over a successful competitor. To do so, he will need to spend several months in Europe, performing due diligence and taking the necessary steps to complete the acquisition. Before leaving, he calls in the presidents of his ten companies and tells them he is leaving each of them the necessary capital to operate their divisions profitably during his absence.

As is often the case, some of his management team harbors a strong dislike for the CEO and constantly searches for ways to undermine his leadership. This, they think, may be the perfect opportunity. When the boss returns, having successfully completed the acquisition, he calls the presidents into his office to get a report on each of the divisions within the corporation. He is particularly interested to find out how much revenue each leader has generated. The first one reports a significant gain, ten times as much as the amount left for operations.

"Wow!" the CEO says, "you are good! You have handled the small things so well that I am going to give you a reward by setting you up with power and authority in ten major cities."

The next one also reports a handsome gain of five times his seed capital.

"All right!" the CEO says. "I will give you power and authority in five major cities."

Then a third president, a noted malcontent whose company perennially ranks on the bottom rungs of performance, speaks up, "I brought back only the original capital that you left. I didn't lose any, but I didn't gain any either. I was afraid of you. I know you are a hard man to deal with. I know you take what isn't yours and you harvest what you did not plant."

"You say I'm a hard man?" the CEO roars. "I'll show you how hard I am. You're fired! Now, take his money and give it to the one who earned the most."

"But sir," one of the other officers gasps, "that's not fair. He's already got more than anyone else."

To which the wise CEO replies, "Let me give you a business principle: Risk your life and get more than you ever dreamed of. Play it safe and end up holding the bag. And for those enemies of mine who used this as an opportunity to rebel against me, get them out of here. I don't want to see their faces around here anymore."

Three Principles

Remember, this parable came from Jesus Himself. In this teaching on business principles, He addressed three points:

- The peril of rebellion.
- The honoring of faithfulness.
- The increase in authority when you are faithful in the little things.

Let's further explore each point.

Rebellion

Luke 19:14 exposes an issue that must be confronted: "But his citizens hated him, and sent a delegation after him, saying, 'We will not have this man to rule over us.' "

I constantly run into Christians wanting to gripe about their boss. Typically, the refrain goes like this: "He's a liar, a cheat, a slave driver, and on top of that, he can't be trusted." And yet they remain on the job, building bitterness within their hearts while sowing seeds of discontent among other employees.

Yet the Bible commands submission to bosses, even the bad ones: "Servants, be submissive to your masters with all fear, not only to the good and gentle, but also to the harsh. For this is commendable, if because of conscience toward God one endures grief, suffering wrongfully. For what credit is it if, when you are beaten for your faults, you take it patiently? But when you do good and suffer, if you take it patiently, this is commendable before God. For to this you were called, because Christ also suffered for us, leaving us an example, that you should follow His steps" (1 Pet. 2:18-21).

Your purpose for being on the job that God has you in right now is to bring the atmosphere of Christ to the place. You can do that much more effectively through obedient submission than rebellious actions. Peter makes it clear that, in our heavenly Father's eyes, you earn more credit for submission to a bad boss than for patiently enduring correction when you are at fault.

Honoring of Faithfulness

In this parable Jesus speaks about the honor of faithfulness. There is something admirable about a trustworthy employee—the person who always shows up on time, who does the job, and who never complains in the midst of carrying out the task. God is calling for faithfulness in our work life as well as our nuclear church life.

Increase in Authority

There is a large segment of our world that will never be won to Christ through nuclear church initiatives. It will not matter how well we run our churches, how efficiently we plan our programs, or how attractive we make our buildings. There are some who will listen only to those whom they consider to be their peers.

Let me remind you of something that you likely know, but that you may not like; however, even if you don't like it, it is still the truth. Here it is: There is a level of authority that comes from being rich. For some reason, when you are rich, others want to know what you think and how you will respond to things. In addition to that, some affluent people will not listen to those whom they consider to be poor or of less social standing. That, of course, is the wrong attitude, but still someone needs to reach them with the gospel, and the only one who can do so will need to be considered as a peer. One of the ways that Christians can reach them is through their success in business. Jesus makes it very clear in the parable in Luke 19 that He honors success. He lifted up the one who had wisely invested the capital and registered a 1,000 percent return on the boss's money.

So may I say to those of you who have achieved a level of success that enables you to do so (without incurring great debt, of course): Buy the new car, move into that gated community in the most posh section of town, or join the country club—not for purposes of show, but to use your influence and authority to reach out to that segment of society that has remained largely untouched by the Body of Christ.

Jesus uses a very interesting word in this story. He says that the one who is faithful with little—in this case, money—gains authority. The authority that He speaks of is governmental authority. I don't believe this necessarily means that you will run for office and hold an elected position. Instead, it may mean that you will have so much authority that those in government will seek your advice and counsel. They will want to make sure that they don't make decisions without your input.

When you think about it, this is the greater authority. When elected officials at various levels in your city, state, or nation seek you out—as they have Chuck Ripka—you have influence. This kind of authority comes through business. Biblical entrepreneurs, I conclude this chapter by issuing a strong call: "Come forth. We need you!"

CHAPTER 10

Reaching Nations

Go therefore and make disciples of all the nations...
(Matthew 28:19).

Berthold and Barbara Becker live in Germany, where he is an astute businessman. Highly respected, over the years he advanced up the ladder of the European division of General Motors. Early in 1986, Jack Smith, who later became president of GM, offered Berthold a top position with the newly established GM Europe central office in Zurich, Switzerland.

However, by 1986 the national prayer movement "Intercessors for Germany" that God had called Berthold and Barbara to pioneer was just taking off. And so it was not totally surprising when shortly after receiving the new offer by GM, the Lord told him to leave GM and go a new way with Him.

In Berthold's words, "The board of GM was shocked about my potential leaving because I was one of their hopeful future top executives. So they offered me one year leave of absence with certain financial benefits and a guarantee to return to a high-level position. The board hoped that I would 'get back to normal' after some time. Six months later, on one day, I received two calls by board members asking how I was and said I could choose the position if I returned.

"The next day the Lord challenged me with Hebrews 10:34-38. Immediately I cut the cord to GM and gave up the benefits of high income, car, house, and other incentives."

Becker accounts for his success at GM Europe because of four things:

1. "My love and dedication to the job and to the product—automobile."

2. "My desire to serve the Lord in my job, like Daniel and other biblical model figures served in their job; and my understanding that my job was God´s life call for me and that I was in that corporation as a Kingdom representative."

3. "Barbara's support as intercessor for me and the company as well as prophetic advisor."

4. "The favor of the Lord and inspiration by the Holy Spirit with regard to management decisions, leading people, and especially with regard to creativity in cost and investment reduction as well as product ideas. In fact, the Lord told me what kind of products were needed in the future, and I was able to influence the design of products in a way that multimillions were saved annually. The effectiveness that comes into an organization when the Holy Spirit is at work is amazing. And in those years, I literally became the 'prophet of the company' and was respected as such."

Even though he did not know at the time where the Lord would lead him, he started a consulting business that within a few years led him to the Ukraine. In going to the Ukraine, it was again the Lord leading him to help ex-Communist nations.

You can imagine a conversation like this between leaders at GM with one of their top prospects.

"If you don't stay with us, what will you do?"

"The Lord is leading me to the Ukraine."

"Are you going to be a missionary? Are you going to plant churches?"

"No, the Lord is leading me as a businessman to the Ukraine to start new businesses."

Although Berthold had no idea what he was going to do there, he began regularly visiting the Ukraine. As he traveled there, he kept asking, "God, what do You want me to do? I know You called me here. What should I do?"

One day, he ate a piece of bread and nearly spit it out on the floor.

"Man, this stuff is awful!" he exclaimed.

In case you weren't aware of it, Germans know how to make good bread. Sensing a need might exist, Berthold investigated the situation and discovered all the bakeries in the Ukraine were run by the government. Now, God instituted government. Without it, we would have anarchy and chaos. Government plays a valuable role in promoting order, peace, and stability. But making bread isn't among its shining functions. So Berthold declared, "I think I'll start some bakeries."

While he didn't know how to bake, Berthold did know how to run a business. So he hired the best baker that he could find and bought some mobile bakeries from the Swiss Army. Although used, this equipment was nearly new. Think about it. The Swiss have never invaded another country in their history, so why did they need mobile bakeries? They didn't, which is why they sold them. Built with the precision of a Swiss watch, they were available for nickels on the dollar.

As time went on, Berthold outfitted ten mobile bakeries and dispatched them throughout the Ukraine as a business model, and used 20 more for humanitarian purposes. This man is a Christian witness, but not while leading a church. Instead, God has led him to start a Kingdom business. Today Berthold and his team regularly lead ex-Communist rulers to Christ when they visit his office to discuss the company's operations.

This Marketplace Minister's business acumen, coupled with his ability to hear from God, has put himself in a blessed position. Not only is his business prospering, but it blesses Ukrainians with a good product and provides jobs to people who, in the long aftermath of the Soviet Union's dissolution, desperately need them.

Strength in Unity

Years ago, my friend Paul Tan related a story that still sticks out in my mind. His partner asked him, "Who is the richest man in the world?" As soon as Paul gave his answer, his partner followed up with, "Is he a Christian? Because the Lord has promised that the wealth of the Gentiles is stored up for us."

Paul said no, but proceeded to discuss other kinds of wealth. He realized later that his words sounded hollow. Dissatisfied with his own response, he prayed, "Lord, why isn't the richest man in the world a Christian? How are You going to reach the nations if we don't even have the wealth of the wicked in our hands?"

After struggling with this issue for several months, one day Paul sensed the Lord's Spirit saying, "Paul, the richest man in the world is a Christian. But it is not a man as you might think. It is My Body. The Body of Christ has more wealth than anyone else. The problem is that My Body is so fragmented that it loses its impact."

When God's people work together, there is tremendous synergy. I have watched for years as the nuclear church has struggled mightily to achieve unity, only to see tepid results. In most cities, the unity of local congregations is confined to small pastoral prayer meetings in quiet places, or an occasional joint venture, expressed by a citywide evangelistic campaign that features a well-known speaker. However, in these last days, the Body of Christ must come together—and business just might be the tool to do it. Peace in the Middle East hasn't come through political agendas. Religious zealotry drives an even deeper wedge between people. But business is a place where we recognize how much we need each other.

In Chapter 4, I noted that a discussion of workplace ministry starts with signs and wonders because it is the clearest biblical sign God gives to His children. The one sign by which the apostle Paul wanted his apostleship judged was its ability to bring the life-changing grace of Jesus Christ to men: "When I was with you, I certainly gave you every proof that I am truly an apostle, sent to you by God Himself. For I patiently did many signs and wonders and miracles among you" (2 Cor. 12:12 NLT).

If a discussion of workplace ministers begins with signs and wonders, then it must end with the goal of reaching whole nations. In Christ's command known as the Great Commission, He called His followers to "Go therefore and make disciples of all the nations..." (Mt. 28:19). Beginning in Genesis, God refers to nations 17 times, including such references as:

Ask of Me, and I will give You the nations for Your inheritance, and the ends of the earth for Your possession (Psalm 2:8).

Let all the nations be gathered together, and let the people be assembled. Who among them can declare this, and show us former things? Let them bring out their witnesses, that they may be justified; or let them hear and say, "It is truth" (Isaiah 43:9).

In the middle of its street, and on either side of the river, was the tree of life, which bore twelve fruits, each tree yielding its fruit every month. The leaves of the tree were for the healing of the nations (Revelation 22:2).

Granted, there are times when the Lord speaks judgment upon nations because of their disobedience, but a detailed inspection of the Bible shows how the heart of God is for the nations of the world—not a particular country, region, or continent, but all the nations. This is best demonstrated through John's vision of Heaven, where he wrote, "After these things I looked, and behold, a great multitude which no one could number, of all nations, tribes, peoples, and tongues, standing before the throne and before the Lamb..." (Rev. 7:9).

Lifting Our Sights

We need to lift our sights to a much higher level in workplace settings and begin to see nations. I will admit that we are still a little weak in this area, but thank God that we are making some headway. I know of many who have this desire firmly planted in their hearts.

I have already spoken about Gunner Olson and the International Christian Chamber of Commerce; what a great work these business operators are doing for the Kingdom of God in many nations.

I just told you about Berthold Becker of Germany. Besides his work in the Ukraine, God is using his business expertise to expand His Kingdom in Mongolia, several African nations, and Israel.

I have spoken of Julian Watts and Richard Fleming in England; and in the U.S., Dennis and Megan Doyle and Jay and Sally Bennett in Minneapolis, Minnesota.

Kyffin Simpson who lives in Barbados is bringing Kingdom Impact throughout the entire region of the Caribbean as well as in the UK and the USA.

All these business leaders, and many others I haven't listed, are operating Kingdom-oriented businesses and are being used by God to bring His presence to nations. In recent years, I have traveled to Kazakhstan and visited with skilled entrepreneurs who have easy access to China. I have worked with a team of relief workers in Afghanistan who have touched several dozens nations to date.

In addition, I recently received an update from my friend, Ed Silvoso, concerning recent advances in his native land of Argentina. Today he is leading a team who is working with every province in the nation. They are distributing goods to the needy, calling together persons of influence, and working with the International

Christian Chamber of Commerce. Their aim is to network Christian businesspeople and inspire, equip, and deploy Marketplace Ministers.

This is personally encouraging because of a meeting we had in the spring of 2002. Over lunch, Ed and I talked about Argentina, which was experiencing considerable turbulence. Four presidents had come and gone in a little over a month. The nation's economy lay in shambles, and despite a revival atmosphere sweeping through its churches, Argentina was in trouble. I remember telling Ed, "You are such a strategist for the Kingdom. Your ideas are being implemented in churches around the world. Ask the Lord for a strategy for your nation. I am sure He will give it to you."

Today, that is happening, not only in Argentina, but in other countries around the world. For the last several years, Mel and Heather Mullen have hosted a conference in Red Deer, Alberta, Canada, known as "Impacting Cities, Influencing Nations." God is using this couple to raise up an army of spiritual leaders in business across Canada. Drawing several thousand people a year to this city of 60,000, several hundred miles north of the Montana border, it recently expanded to Montreal and Ottawa. Plans are being made to eventually penetrate all the provinces in the nation.

While Mel is a pastor, he recognizes the need for leadership outside traditional church boundaries. For example, he has been mentoring Mike Furst, a young businessman in his congregation. Recently he named Furst a "Marketplace Minister" for the church and publicly recognized him as a minister to the business world in their city and for their nation.

Early in 2004, I came in contact with Rick and Sue Seeberger, a couple whom the Lord is using to reach businesspersons in Paraguay, the Caribbean, Mexico, and the United States. Their heart is for changing the nations, but their tools are not traditional evangelism and church planting. Instead, their focus is on teaching character and equipping people to walk in integrity, where their word remains reliable and truthful regardless of circumstances.

After spending time trying to work within traditional nuclear church structures, Rick took his ministry (business) to the business community and discovered a receptive audience for these teachings. I see these examples as a signal that the nations of our world are being prepared right now to receive a Kingdom message.

And yet, while I am encouraged, I am not satisfied. While I know we are on track, in this particular area I believe we need to greatly increase our faith, energy level, and passion to push forward and reach the world for Christ.

Standing for the Kingdom

In America, we have watched for years (with some fear and trepidation) as militant Muslims from the Middle East have emigrated to the U.S. Obviously, they did not come as "missionaries" with an evangelistic agenda; we have known what was in their hearts. They came as businesspeople with a purpose to establish their presence in our land, with a desire to penetrate and ultimately take control. They are strongly militant in support of their cause, but their platform has been business.

Likewise, it is time for Kingdom-minded businesspeople to stand up for Christ, not only in the workplace, but in developing strategies that have the power to impact entire nations. Do you work for a multinational corporation? What I mean by that is one that has offices in several countries or that conducts trade in multiple nations. If so, start to exert your spiritual authority in prayer over the nations represented by your company.

Do you feel a call from God to be a missionary? Carefully consider the modern trend toward "business as mission." There are still numerous places today where you cannot go as a missionary, church planter, or evangelist, but that will welcome you as a business leader. God gave you an entrepreneurial spirit; now is the time for it to come forth to bless your nation and others around the globe.

During one visit to the Middle East, no one knew that I was a Christian, much less a former pastor. Yet, they welcomed my teaching as a business consultant. Although circumstances dictated avoiding conventional biblical terminology, during a seminar several other Christian businesspersons and I were able to teach biblical principles. The result was souls entering God's Kingdom—not because of preaching, but through serving as living examples. At the end of our short visit, several Middle Easterners decided to follow Christ. They made such comments as, "If you guys are Christians, I would like to be one also." In rebuilding the Middle East, God is calling for us to come in less traditional, yet practical and anointed ways, to touch those nations for His Kingdom.

Every sign demonstrated by workplace ministers needs to be harnessed for the reaching of whole nations. When Jesus told us that we would do the works that He did, but that we would also do even greater works (see Jn. 14:12), could it be that He was referring to miracles that could impact entire nations? Do you have enough faith for that kind of miracle? Use your God-given authority to bring about changes in nations.

Biblical entrepreneurs need to start thinking in broader terms, including how they can establish multinational businesses that can impact the nations for God. As you are praying for the coming transfers of wealth, realize that much of this is for the nations, not for personal gain. For those who listen closely to what God is saying today, I am confident that He is speaking to you about nations. When thinking of transforming societies, we cannot be content with touching only America's inner cities. Instead, we must begin to think in terms of whole nations. Christ's call is not just to reach people or cities, but to disciple whole nations. We cannot be content until that goal is on the heart of every Marketplace Minister.

The signs of a workplace minister are many and varied, but when considering them as a whole we can envision the God-given mandate to reach entire nations. This will not happen by "stand alone" leaders working in obscurity or from atop a pedestal of pride. This will happen when we see the Body of Christ coming together in harmony and purpose. It will happen when we lay down individual agendas for the greater work of the gospel.

As I mentioned, I don't have that perfect illustration of nation-reaching Marketplace Ministers to discuss as of this writing. Still, I trust that some of you reading these words are writing it in your own life experience today. I know this is the heart of God, and I know that many of you are following hard after Him in this way. I speak to such obedient followers of Christ in a prophetic sense: You will be used by God in these coming days to bring about changes in whole nations. Expect the strategies to come. When they do, join with your brothers and sisters to see that they are implemented.

CHAPTER 11

Marketplace Minister in Action

And these signs will follow those who believe: in My name they will cast out demons; they will speak with new tongues; they will take up serpents; and if they drink anything deadly, it will by no means hurt them; they will lay hands on the sick, and they will recover (Mark 16:17-18).

In this Scripture passage, Jesus refers to God giving power to His followers. This supernatural power enables them to perform miraculous deeds. I am confident that such signs will become evident in the lives of thousands of Marketplace Ministers. I have outlined seven of these signs; there are undoubtedly more. However, these are the ones the Lord indicated and prompted me to write about. Over the next several years, we will see increasing numbers of workplace ministers. As they emerge, these signs will accompany them.

About three years ago, when I first started meditating on—and considering the reality of—these anointed Marketplace Ministers, I knew of only a few. But as my travels expanded from city to city and nation to nation, I started encountering increasing numbers of this new breed of minister. Not only did I locate them, but they already knew who they were because God had been speaking to them. I remember a conversation with Ken Beaudry, a business leader in Elk River, Minnesota, the city I wrote about in Chapter 9. After observing the developments in this city and his life, I remarked, "Ken, I believe you are a marketplace apostle."

"I know it," he replied. "The Lord told me that some time back."

It shouldn't amaze any of God's followers that the Lord had been speaking to many individuals about His call on their life long before anyone else recognized it.

Practical Helps

I want to include some practical guidance in this book. Not only do we need to know the signs of Marketplace Ministers, we need to have ways to recognize these leaders. I talked to the Lord about this and asked Him how I could best explain this to readers. In response, God revealed that there were four primary ways to recognize workplace ministers:

1. *They carry an unusual authority in their sphere of influence.*

If we look only within the nuclear church, we will miss these members of God's powerful workforce. In Christendom, we have typically found our leaders in the nuclear church, but workplace ministers will carry authority in the place where their influence will be most keenly felt. Most sociological thinkers now identify eight major spheres of influence in the world:

- Religion.
- Family.
- Government/law.
- Health.
- Education.
- Business.
- Entertainment/media.

- Science and technology (The latter was added recent-ly because of major advances in this field.)

This means we will find God's Marketplace Ministers in education, who will command authority in the educational system. The same will be true in the church, family, government, medicine, business, media, and science. God is giving His children the authority to operate in each of these spheres of influence. As Christians, we will not find ourselves making an impact on the world until we have identified, equipped, and released leaders in each of these disciplines. For too long, we have tried to accomplish the task of winning (and discipling) converts within the structure of the local church. With some obvious exceptions, this has not worked too well.

Now think of your city. Likely the leaders in the local church arena are becoming identified and acknowledged. In recent years we have made small strides toward identifying the leaders in the business community, which I believe is foundational to moving forward with our task. However, after identifying them, we must train and release the God-ordained leaders in each sphere of influence and each city and region. The good news is: God is already speaking to them, calling them, and preparing them for the next wave of transformation.

To find and identify them, look for the authority. Actor Mel Gibson is a prime example. He received a vision from the Lord, and despite tremendous persecution and second-guessing that he was throwing away his career, he filmed *The Passion of the Christ*. Within less than two months of its premiere, it had passed $350 million in box office receipts, ranking it among history's most popular movies. Gibson was able to carry this off because of the high level of authority God gave him. Now that he has succeeded, his authority level is even higher.

You will find the same to be true in your life. Walk in the authority that the Lord has given you, and you will succeed in fulfilling His purpose for your life. As you move into the success arena, your authority level will increase. In Matthew 28:18, Jesus said that all authority had been given to Him, both in Heaven and on earth. He has chosen to pass it on to today's workplace ministers.

2.   *They are involved in mentoring and equipping others.*

A study of the five ministry gifts in Ephesians 4:11 shows that God gave them to us as foundational gifts, used to train and equip others. When you examine this verse, you will note that these five ministry gifts were given to the Church to equip saints for:

- The work of the ministry.
- The edifying (uplifting and encouraging) of the Body of Christ.

Workplace ministers must also see their responsibility in training up others to follow them, assist them, and take the Kingdom of God into the sphere of influence where they carry authority. Since the workplace is the place of ministry for these leaders, their task is to equip other saints to carry out ministry there. When that is done, it is edifying and encouraging. When a person steps into his or her call and purpose, it is of great personal benefit and a boost for the larger Body of Christ. Hopefully, you can see that it is inadequate to confine ministerial training to nuclear church settings. If we continue to operate in that fashion, we will continue to train only one kind of minister.

I call upon Marketplace Ministers to mentor and equip the believers who are following you. I purposely use the word "mentor" for reasons spelled out by Rick Seeberger, the leader I mentioned in Chapter 10. He heads an organization called BFCI (Business for Change International), and in a training manual titled, *Dynamics of the Marketplace Church*, Rick says:

As a Master Trainer, there are five dimensions of relationship impact:

Dimension One – Teaching (imparting knowledge).

The difference between a good teacher and a bad teacher is that a bad teacher teaches a subject; however a good teacher teaches the student. It is what is "caught" that is more important than what is "taught."

Dimension Two – Counseling.

A counselor is given the opportunity (a window) into another person's life at the request of the person being counseled. Marriage and financial counseling are examples. The counselor oftentimes is afforded limited access to the person's "whole life." A good counselor helps a person improve their capacity for change.

Dimension Three – Coaching.

A coach is called upon to help a person improve specific skills and even to improve other aspects of life. A coach is dedicated to seeing individuals grow and to develop their life potential. As a form of Coaching, the next two dimensions relate to the type of disciplines or programs a person is developing toward.

Dimension Four – Discipling.

A person who is Discipling another person is normally teaching and overseeing a person in the fundamental character, knowledge and skills needed to function within a specific program. For example, Jesus called twelve men and discipled them into His "program" of life and ministry. Today, many churches have discipleship programs to teach people what it is to be a follower of Christ. The challenge is that discipleship often focuses people into a church mindset rather than on life purpose. Consequently, the vast majority of Christians see their ministry *inside* the church, instead of in the *outreach* of the church. At some point, people need to be sent out to prove their capacity to reproduce.

Dimension Five – Mentoring.

Mentoring can involve all the prior dimensions and has a primary focus on reproducing the essential ingredients of

character, knowledge, and skills. In addition, a commitment inherent to mentoring is the dedication to releasing
the person after they are mentored. Effective mentoring
focuses the mentor on reproducing the capacity he/she
has into the life of the one being mentored. A person
requesting a mentor is asking the mentor to equip them
with the necessary ingredients needed to achieve the goals
they've set for themselves. Examples would be a master
carpenter equipping an apprentice; a medical doctor
mentoring an intern; Paul and Timothy. Mentoring focuses on equipping and releasing. The disciples went on to
become apostles (foundation layers) without Jesus physi-
cally continuing to oversee their activities.[1]

This kind of training will come from Marketplace Ministers as
they reproduce themselves and release these "mentees" into all
spheres of influence. If there is a failing in the modern church, it
has been its tendency to withdraw from society. When Christian
influence diminishes in the world, the world gets progressively
worse. It is time that Christians make their presence known and felt
in societies from Boston to Beijing.

3.   *They are causing, or are already involved in, city or nation-
     wide transformation.*

I spoke about this at length in the last chapter, but it merits
repeating because I believe this is so high on God's agenda. If you
are not involved in some form of initiative to transform cities or
nations, you are missing the point of your calling and destiny in
Christ. To put it bluntly: If you are not involved in such an effort,
you are not a Marketplace Minister. The first step in the right direction is a change of mind-set. You know that you are called by God
to serve Him in your sphere of influence. Now, begin to ask Him to
give you favor in a wider range, as far as the borders of your nation.

I have discovered that many Marketplace Ministers know they
are in the ministry, but have not been affirmed in this task by their
local congregation. As a result of this lack of recognition, many

have either done nothing with regard to their call or have worked in isolation and ineffectiveness. Now that you are being affirmed in your true calling, take it to the level that God wants to give to you. This change of mind-set includes the acceptance of your call, embracing its mandate, and fulfilling God's purpose.

One example of societal transformation has occurred in the South American country of Paraguay. This nation is being transformed by God's Kingdom through a marketplace initiative formed by Business for Change International. According to Rick Seeberger, this is what they are seeing:

> In July of 1997, we began a Strategic Training Initiative in the nation of Paraguay to establish a Marketplace church effort. In March 1999, we formed a Champions of Change Team (mostly of non-Christians, but individuals who wanted to see a meaningful change in their country) and the next month we formed the first Leadership Institute in the nation.
>
> Today, members of Champions of Change Team are in the process of Nation Building (transforming the nation) and six of them are in strategic positions politically. One is the new president of the nation, another is the mayor of the capital city, two are senior advisors to the president, and others hold influential positions in the nation.
>
> This approach has afforded us the opportunity to train and equip leaders within government departments, businesses of all sizes, and other organizations from the public and private sectors. The impact from these efforts now as the potential to reach millions.[2]

4.   *They are forming "church" in the workplace.*

As many look beyond the sanctuary walls to take a broader view of "church," we will see new expressions of Christianity in the workplace. In the past, these have been mostly copies of the nuclear church. Typically, a few followers of Christ banded together for a

135

prayer group or Bible study over lunch, meeting behind closed doors so they could "get away from all the sinners" and "have some good fellowship." I have no doubt that these groups have served a valuable service to participants. I am grateful to the Lord for allowing this sort of activity to take place. However, if we are to impact the workplace, there must be new congregational forms to encompass wider corporate settings.

The one thing that seems to be missing in most workplace ministries is the "prophetic," meaning both the ability to hear God's voice and the attention given to that aspect of supernatural gifting. Without hearing from the Lord, we move on in our strength and power, continuing to design fleshly programs that lack supernatural power. With it, we are able to move into the spheres that God intends for us.

Church in the workplace may have the same feel as the nuclear church, but the form will be different. I encourage you to pray with the door—and your eyes—open. Learn to talk to God as if you were talking to your best friend. Let "church" be a part of who you are on a daily basis, not just at a special meeting or a specific meeting place. Recognize the presence of God in the workplace. Access His presence and power in the normal, daily flow of work life.

If you can recognize the daily presence of God, you will know that you are clothed with the Spirit of God. That means that our human weakness is covered and that everything contrary to the mind of God is destroyed. It means that we are filled with the Spirit of God, so that we never need to go anywhere but to Him and His Word for answers, whatever the circumstances. When we start to act like we are the Church in daily life, we will recognize that Christ is in us. That means that any of His promises can be appropriated in your office, plant, or sales venue. God has put within us such power and revelation that the possibilities of what can be done are endless. There isn't anything that you can imagine that is greater than what man can accomplish through Him.

In Pat Gilsinger's book, *Balancing Your Family, Faith and Work*, Intel's chief technology officer talks candidly about living for Christ at work: "I have taken every major chip, project, organization, business or technology that I've worked on for over twenty years at Intel before the throne of God. I suggest you do so with your work as well."[3]

Gilsinger also talks about opportunities to share God at work:

- Your first witness in the workplace is being a great employee. If you don't do that, you will diminish any level of witness that you might have.

- Your second witness is your lifestyle and ethics. Do you conduct your life with the highest of morals and ethics, or do you casually participate in corrupt or questionable behavior? Do you participate in crude discussions or joking? Do people see you having your personal devotions during your breaks and lunch hours?

- Third, you will get opportunities to express concern for others in a godly and genuine way. If a coworker is ill or has lost a family member, an "I'll be thinking of you and praying for you," a gift of flowers, or a genuine, "I'll come over and help you during your time of need" will speak volumes.

- Finally, you may be afforded the occasional opportunity to witness verbally to others. This needs to be done with great prudence, lest you ever gain the reputation of using work time to proselytize. This is also why I put such emphasis on being a "great employee" and putting your professional character above reproach. You must be even more cautious not to allow your position as a supervisor to place pressure on a subordinate in this regard. You should never witness during work time, only during breaks or off time.[4]

There is great joy in being at the place where we can count on being in the presence of His power. Knowing the presence and power of God at your workplace will lead you to the place where victory is assured. As I read my Bible, I find that Jesus always blessed the work of His disciples. God has given us a clear mandate to know that our work is our ministry. Now it is up to us to appropriate that power and purpose and know that God can do anything with us. Any problem that might be faced in the workplace has a solution in God. This is church in the workplace—not a closed-door prayer meeting, but an open-door invitation to the power of God to move in every situation.

So now, Marketplace Ministers, it is up to you. The signs are clear, and they are available to you:

1. Signs and wonders.
2. Authority.
3. Bondage breakers.
4, Wealth transfer.
5. Hearing the voice of God.
6. Biblical entrepreneurs.
7. Reaching nations.

This is your mandate—to use a business term, your job description. Still, don't get hung up on titles; others will recognize you because of your character. I recently heard a businessman say, "Gifts are common, and free. Character is rare, and costly." In short, character is:

- That rare quality that causes people to trust you even when they don't know you well.

- A sign of integrity that causes even your enemies to know that you are true to your word.

- That inner peace that rests on you at night because you know that you have walked in God's ways throughout the day.

- Who you are when no one else is watching.

Let God develop authentic, godly character in you so that you are ready to be used in transforming the nations of the world.

Endnotes

1. Rick Seeberger, *Dynamics of a Marketplace Church* (El Paso, TX.: BFCI Learning Systems, Ltd., 2003) 3-4, used by permission.

2. Ibid, 8.

3. Pat Gelsinger, *Balancing Your Family, Faith & Work* (Colorado Springs, CO: Life Journey, an imprint of Cook Communications Ministries, 2003) 126.

4. Ibid, 138-139.

CHAPTER 12

Developing Marketplace Ministers

"Give me wisdom and knowledge to rule them properly, for who is able to govern this great nation of Yours?" God said to Solomon, "Because your greatest desire is to help your people, and you did not ask for personal wealth and honor or the death of your enemies or even a long life, but rather you asked for wisdom and knowledge to properly govern My people, I will certainly give you the wisdom and knowledge you requested. And I will also give you riches, wealth, and honor such as no other king has ever had before you or will ever have again!"
(2 Chronicles 1:10-12 NLT)

When the state of Virginia joined the 1861 revolt against the United States, Robert E. Lee sided with the South. Despite fighting on the losing side in the Civil War, this general's fame has long outlived him. Lee is still lauded for his valiant leadership of an outmanned, out-equipped, and out-spent Confederacy. Ironically, U.S. President Abraham Lincoln offered Lee command of all Union forces after the battle at Fort Sumter that sparked the Civil War. But the skilled military leader declared that he would follow his native state "with my sword and if need be, my life."

Far less known to the casual observer of history is fellow Virginian George Thomas, like Lee, a graduate of West Point Military Academy. Soon after Fort Sumter erupted, Virginia's governor offered Thomas the command of all state artillery forces. Most Virginians, particularly his family, assumed he would side with the South. But in the spring of 1861 he announced he would remain loyal to the Union. Declared Thomas "I took an oath at West Point to defend the Constitution and to serve my country. I do not break my oaths."

Thomas went on to become a great general, rising to the rank of Union army commander in Tennessee and Georgia. He directed a brilliant defensive stand at the battle of Chickamauga in 1863 and fought with General William Sherman in Atlanta. Historians rank him among the top Union generals. At the end of the war, Congress passed a resolution in his honor. Promoted to major general in the army, Thomas received the command of his choice—the Department of the Pacific, headquartered in San Francisco.

However, he paid a high price for his decision. Loyalty to his country earned him scorn at home. Not only did he sever ties with his native state, but with his own flesh and blood. When Thomas died from a massive stroke in 1870, nearly 10,000 people attended his funeral in New York. But not a single member of his family attended. Asked later why they did not come, one of his sisters replied, "As far as we're concerned, our brother died in 1861."[1]

What would drive a man to risk deeply rooted family ties to uphold his nation's honor? I believe it lies in West Point's Cadet Honor Code, simply defined as: "A cadet will not lie, cheat, steal, or tolerate those who do." On a behavioral level, the Code represents a simple standard for all cadets. On a developmental plane, West Point expects that all cadets will strive to live above the minimum standard of behavior. As leaders, they are to develop the kind of commitment to ethical principles that guides their moral actions.

West Point's core mission is to develop leaders of character for the United States Army. A leader of character knows what is right and possesses the moral courage to act on that knowledge. Principles of truthfulness, fairness, respect for others, and a personal commitment to maintaining values constitute that fundamental ideal known as the Spirit of the Code. A leader of character will apply the Spirit of the Code when facing sticky ethical dilemmas.

The conduct expected of military cadets ranks far above that demonstrated in recent years in businesses, corporations, and government agencies. In certain business sectors, discussing honesty, integrity, or ethics prompts laughter. Worse, I have discovered that even in Christian circles simply keeping your word is not a given. I long ago stopped trying to keep track of broken promises made to me in churches.

Given this reality, it is no wonder that Christ's simple command, "But let your 'Yes' be 'Yes,' and your 'No,' 'No' " (Mt. 5:37a), is seldom applied in the business world. By the way, if you have become so enamored of relativism that you think I am being "legalistic" or "pushy" about the need to honor your word, look at how Jesus finished verse 37: "For whatever is more than these is from the evil one."

Code of Values

The question is: What can be done about this sad state of affairs? As followers of Christ in business, I believe we all need to adopt a code that we will operate by, regardless of circumstances. As I compiled a list of admirable values, it became quite lengthy. I suppose you could shorten it by designing some subcategories, but I recommend not editing it and thereby not permitting some questionable actions to slip through the cracks.

The military code of honor includes four traits:

1. No lying.
2. No cheating.
3. No stealing.
4. No toleration of those who do.

Recently we had a strategic planning session for our consulting organization. From a list of 16 we chose four as the ones we would emphasize as our core values. They include integrity, reliability, joy, and servanthood.

Integrity: We want to integrate truth into everything we do.

Well-known management experts James Kouzes and Barry Posner are the authors of *The Leadership Challenge*. Often quoted is a worldwide survey they conducted of several thousand people, seeking to identify the most desirable traits of a good leader. *Honesty* ranked at the top, far ahead of the runner-up, *competence*.

Ask almost anyone on the street about the highly publicized falls of Enron, WorldCom, or Martha Stewart, and you are likely to hear responses about how people in these enterprises lacked integrity. Interestingly, three of the Ten Commandments (see Ex. 20:15-17) are directly associated with integrity:

Number 8: "You shall not steal" (verse 15).

Number 9: "You shall not bear false witness against your neighbor (verse 16).

Number 10: "You shall not covet your neighbor's house; you shall not covet your neighbor's wife, nor his male servant, nor his female servant, nor his ox, nor his donkey, nor anything that is your neighbor's" (verse 17).

When I speak of *integrity*, I am referring to both the popular and classical meanings of the word. The popular usage is to consider *integrity* and *honesty* as synonyms, so *truthfulness* becomes the primary way in which most view this word. Certainly there is no excuse for a lack of truthfulness in our lives at home or at work.

However, the classical definition of *integrity* is derived from the Latin and speaks of wholeness or completeness. From this Latin root we get words like *integer* (whole numbers) and *integration*. It speaks of cohesiveness and oneness, of a bringing together.

I like to think of integrity as the quality of living on the outside, like you think and really are on the inside. Integrity is the integration of all the aspects of your life into one cohesive lifestyle. When integrity is present, we act the same way at work as we do at a worship service, or the same way at home as we do on vacation.

A glaring problem in many societies is the establishment of different rules for work and home. The woman who would never allow her children to lie has developed a lifestyle of lying in order to make sales at work. The man who would never cheat on his wife regularly cheats on his income tax returns. The church member who professes to believe in Christ thinks nothing of violating copyright laws by burning CDs or copying MP3 files to pass along software and music to friends.

Integrity requires a company to communicate the same message to the general public that it does to its employees. It also requires that a company does for its employees what it promised them at the time of their hiring. Ever felt disillusioned because a raise or other promised perk somehow never materialized? And the explanation of why included the reasonable sounding excuse of an economic downturn or company restructuring?

The lack of integrity (wholeness) also promotes a compartmentalization of our lives. In other words, we separate our behavior into secular and spiritual realms. If you adopt different rules for your spiritual life than for your secular existence, it demonstrates a lack of integrity. Why? Because a person of integrity has integrated his or her values into a pattern of wholeness.

When you think of integrity, do you think of a person who lives up to that standard? I do. And I want others to think of me in that way. Without a doubt, truthfulness is part of integrity, but so is living up to one's commitments.

Reliability: You can count on us.

This quality is closely associated with integrity. A reliable person is trustworthy. This person will protect confidential information, can always be depended upon, and provides others the confidence that he will finish the job, no matter how long it takes or how much work it requires.

I remember a game we used to play as a child. Dad would stand behind me and say, "Fall back and I will catch you." And he always did. He was teaching me two things: 1) to trust him and 2) reliability. I could count on him to keep his word. I knew my father as a man who always kept his word, whether at home, in business, or other aspects of his life. I once saw an evil derivative of this game in which a cruel father let his child fall to the ground. His sneering comment: "Never trust anyone."

While it is true that some people cannot be trusted, I prefer to believe the best about others. I strive to develop relationships with those who can be trusted. I have often heard the philosophy that since you cannot trust others, make sure you protect yourself with extensive legal documents. However, what I have discovered is that if you cannot trust someone, a $500-an-hour attorney cannot alter the outcome.

My belief is that change must come from the inside and be evidenced in outward actions. A myriad of rules, laws, and restrictions do little to change behavior. After all, if the Ten Commandments would have persuaded everyone to obey God's law, there wouldn't have been a need for Jesus to come to earth.

Those who boast about keeping all the rules are usually breaking a few behind everyone's back. Better to be a quiet person of reliability who can be counted on at all times. Reliability should be an assumed quality for Christian business leaders. Showing ourselves to be reliable people can change the future. If you have stumbled in this area, today is not too late to establish a new habit.

Joy: Let's have fun at work.

We chose joy as one of the core values for our company because we believe that work should be enjoyable. Since numerous polls reveal considerable employee dissatisfaction with work environments, we want to change the atmosphere by helping restore joy in the work-place. Nehemiah 8:10b teaches that "the joy of the Lord is your strength." In fact, there are more than 180 references to *joy* or *joy-ful* in the Bible.

Can you imagine a workplace filled with joy? Everyone is having fun, which lowers stress, increases productivity, and sends laughter echoing down the halls. In my mind, joy represents more than the pleasure of making money. It is a place where purpose, direction, and destiny are a part of work. One of our newest associates told me that working with us was fun "because I sense this is a part of who I am and what I was created for."

When you are able to use your talents in the way that the Lord intended and fulfill the purposes for which He created you, you will find joy. If you carry the joy of the Lord in your life, I believe that you can make a much greater Kingdom impact. This includes coworkers, supervisors, suppliers, customers, and other associates.

Imagine a Christian walking into work who is mad at the world. He might fling open the door, kick the tires on his car, and respond to a coworker's "Good morning" with a belligerent, "What's good about it?" After striding into his office and sitting down, Mr. Grouch says, "Now Lord, use me today." It is not likely he will make an impact—at least, not for God's Kingdom.

Now imagine another worker, full of the joy of the Lord. Happy with life, she has been listening to praise music en route to work. She walks into the office with a spring in her step and sings out, "Good morning, everybody. What a beautiful day. I am so happy. What a great day to be alive. I am so excited about what is going to happen." When she sits down at her desk and prays, "Now Lord, use me," something is bound to occur.

BrainyDictionary.com defines joy as: "The passion or emotion excited by the acquisition or expectation of good; pleasurable feelings or emotions caused by success, good fortune, and the like, or by a rational prospect of possessing what we love or desire; gladness; exhilaration of spirits; delight." Can you think of a joyful person?

Why not be one yourself and see the strength that the Lord will add to you.

Servanthood: We emphasize being servant leaders.

I first heard the term "servant leader" from a businessman in our congregation in 1979. I liked the term then and I like it even more today. Of course, the idea is not new. Nearly 2,000 years ago Jesus advised that "whoever desires to become great among you shall be your servant" (Mk. 10:43).

More recently a number of management and leadership books on the topic of servant leadership have appeared. One notable title is *Servant Leadership: A Journey into the Nature of Legitimate Power and Greatness* by Robert K. Greenleaf. First published in 1977 and reissued 25 years later, in these prophetic essays Greenleaf defines servant leadership as a practical philosophy. In his eyes, it should replace traditional, autocratic decision-making with a holistic, ethical approach.

This highly influential book has been embraced by cutting-edge management teams across the world. Yet in this modern-day ethical quagmire, which has prompted VISA CEO Dee Hock to label our "era of massive institutional failure," Greenleaf's seminal work is needed in mainstream business circles more than ever. *Servant Leadership* helps leaders find their true power and moral authority.

Building on the principles that Greenleaf introduced, consultant Ken Blanchard wrote *Servant Leader*. The best-selling coauthor of *The One-Minute Manager*, Blanchard and coauthor Phil Hodges reveal the meaning of servant leadership modeled after Jesus Christ. As Blanchard says at his popular "Lead Like Jesus" seminars, "We serve. That's what Jesus mandates. It's clear. The secret of great leaders is they serve."[2]

Such teaching helps business leaders realize that teams are more powerful than the sum of the individuals and to recognize people as appreciating assets. Blanchard demonstrated this ethic when his company faced staggering losses in the aftermath of the 9-11 terrorist attacks. Instead of the knee-jerk method of slashing staff, he opened the books to everyone and asked for ideas on cutting costs. Not only did they recover, but in the middle of October 2004 they had met their fiscal goals for the entire year. The firm rewarded employees with a mid-winter trip to Hawaii.

"Some of these people have never flown," Blanchard told a seminar audience in Louisville, Kentucky. "They're pumped up."[3]

A servant leader is someone who wants to help others succeed. Picture someone who puts others first, who does not spend inordinate amounts of time talking about or promoting him or herself. According to principles outlined in Scripture, this is the sign of authentic leadership. Motivational speaker Zig Ziglar has popularized the phrase, "See you at the top." We would tweak that to say, "Serve your way to the top."

Other Key Values

While our company chose integrity, reliability, joy, and servanthood for our guiding principles, there is a long list of other values that you may choose to set a vision for your business. Among them are:

Righteousness

This word is often associated with Christianity since it has to do with God and our response to Him. Although that is true, righteousness simply means to do what is right. When a person exhibits righteousness, he or she is always thinking of doing the right thing. Sometimes this will fall outside expected performance standards established by the company. When I say "outside standards," I do not mean to imply breaking any rules. Rather, I mean going beyond the minimum—walking the extra mile, as Jesus advised in Matthew 5:41.

I once had an employee who had been with our organization longer than anyone else. While an excellent employee, her health had steadily deteriorated, forcing her to take increasing amounts of sick leave. When she had exhausted all of her leave time, including vacation, personal time, and anything else I could think of to excuse her, I told her, "Just take the time you need to get well. Your job will be here when you are ready."

Ironically, she did not need the money. She needed the job. It gave her hope and a reason to live. As she struggled to recover, I told her she could set her own hours and design her tasks. In this case, it was just the right thing to do. A boss who embraces righteousness will not hunt for rules in an effort to make someone conform. Likewise, employees who do right will not be content with simply fulfilling their own job description. Instead, they will find the target as they strive for righteousness.

Sharing

Just as my father taught me to trust him when I was a young boy, parents endeavor to teach the trait of sharing to their toddlers. We encourage and reward them for sharing, be that toys or candy. While we may now be responsible adults, building lives that impact for the Kingdom of God, sharing is still a commendable activity.

The Bible speaks of sharing in many ways; sharing resources is one. There is also a need to share credit for a job that involves multiple team members, profits that many helped create, and the workload, especially the part that is fun and brings satisfaction.

Justice or fairness

In his new book, *Joy at Work*, Dennis Bakke tells that one of the shared values of the company he founded was fairness. He writes,

> When it comes to "fairness" I think we chose the right value but the wrong word. In my lectures, I often ask people to complete the sentence: Fairness means treating everyone _____. Ninety-five percent of the people I ask respond, "the same." I usually respond, "I mean just the opposite." The word "justice" better describes the standard that we set for ourselves at AES

[the multinational energy company from which he has since retired].

I like the traditional Jewish definition of justice: "To each person what he deserves, to each one what is appropriate." If I combine this definition with an assumption that each person is unique, I logically complete the question this way: "Fairness or justice means treating everyone differently."[4]

Everyone has heard the statement: "Nobody gets special treatment around here." I suggest changing that to: "Everyone gets special treatment around here."

Other desirable values might include:

Self-control

There must be restraint in all areas of potential self-indulgence. For example, when we do not take care of our bodies through proper eating and exercise, we open the door for the devil to hinder our productivity in business and spiritual matters. This can extend to other areas, such as fighting the temptation to take the easy way out, or refusing to cut corners even if the customer will never notice or doesn't appreciate our efforts.

Patience

Many people I know expect instant results; if something beneficial doesn't happen immediately, they quit. I have seen this with prophetic words that stirred great excitement. A week or month later, when nothing had changed, the person forgot about the message and started seeking other answers. I have seen sparkling business ideas tossed aside because they didn't result in overnight success. Remember that patience is one of the manifestations of the fruit of the Holy Spirit (see Gal. 5:22-23).

Humility

As with servanthood, this is the biblical way to greatness. First Peter 5:5b says that "God resists the proud, but gives grace to the humble." Just think of how you responded in the past to the boss who acted as if he knew everything and looked down on you as a peon—compared to one who asked for your feedback, valued your opinion, and complimented your contributions to the organization.

Faithfulness

In a business setting, this speaks to our confidence in God to fulfill what He has promised, as well as faithfulness to the tasks the Lord has called us to complete. It refers to our constant allegiance to the people we are connected to by ties of love, gratitude, or honor. Like a husband is faithful to his wife, or a wife to a husband, so we all must be faithful to the call of God on our lives in the marketplace.

Efficiency

Early in my ministry to business leaders, I saw little outward response when I prayed for them. Based on my years of experience as a pastor, I was accustomed to getting some kind of response, whether tears, laughter, a smile, or just a slight shrug of the shoulders. But now I was getting nothing; it felt like trying to carve a statue of stone with a plastic butter knife.

Finally, I asked the Lord about it. He replied, "This is My business-efficient anointing." I interpreted that to mean I should stop measuring my effectiveness by the traditional, emotional response. Businesspersons are practical; they are geared for action and finding solutions. As they respond to God's direction, He helps them implement His answers. I believe that the Lord will help us to be more efficient, helping us work smarter instead of harder. Because of God's grace, I believe the day will come that we will accomplish twice the work in half the time.

Goodness

Another manifestation of the fruit of the Spirit, this is the simple quality of being good in all of its various senses: kindness, virtue, excellence, character, giving, caring, and conduct. Goodness is visible in the community, just as selfish, tight-fisted business operators don't go unnoticed.

I once heard a story about a deacon in a Baptist church. Although his social standing and wealth earned him a seat of honor in the church, he was known around town as a conniving thief who would leave no stone unturned if he thought it would bring him a fast buck. Remarking on his status in the church, one non-member said, "If that's the kind of people you allow to serve as leaders, I have no interest in coming there."

Responsibility

This is another way of discussing reliability and trust. The responsible person is the kind of individual who is likely to respond, who will answer when called, or will return calls even if he is busy at the time. He will demonstrate responsibility in all areas, including finances, conduct, time, and other aspects of business. Responsibility involves a degree of accountability on the part of the person concerned, such as the person who answers to stockholders, a board of directors, or employees.

Stewardship

This value almost made our top four list. We are to be good stewards of all that God has entrusted to our care. As Jesus said after He told His disciples the parable of the unjust steward, "He who is faithful in what is least is faithful also in much; and he who is unjust in what is least is unjust also in much" (Lk. 16:10).

Perseverance

Several years ago, I heard a story about two large dogs that regularly passed the house where a much smaller bulldog lived. Each day they went by the house, the bulldog emerged to challenge them. They were larger and outnumbered him two to one, so they always won the fight. Still, the little bulldog always came back for more. Finally, the bigger dogs would no longer walk by the house. Whenever they drew near the other dog, they would whimper and cry, and run back home. The perseverance of the smaller bulldog won. Likewise, there will be times when the task seems too big, but if we tackle it with a bulldog's tenacity, we will win.

In Conclusion

I have devoted a considerable amount of space to my discussion of the core values, ethics, and character we as business leaders must exhibit. I do so for a purpose. Think of the plethora of companies that have fallen into bankruptcy or disgrace in recent years because of a lack of ethics.

The one trait that all these business leaders had in common: They were brilliant. Many emulated their business practices. They had money, far more than most people on this planet will ever dream of seeing. They possessed tremendous expertise and highly trained and qualified staffs. And yet Enron and a long list of others have fallen from their lofty perch.

Why? They didn't have the core values to motivate them, keep them on track, and check their indulgence for more, more, and more. They lost sight of the overriding core value of love, which seeks to serve others instead of self. As the apostle Paul wrote, "Though I speak with the tongues of men and of angels, but have not love, I have become sounding brass or a clanging cymbal" (1 Cor. 13:1).

South Dakota's Tom Daschle retired from the Senate at the end of 2004 after losing his bid for reelection. Just before departing, he talked about the moving experience of an unnamed colleague bidding him farewell and saying, "I love you." While that remark generated scorn from the conservative political commentators who cheered his defeat, their views blinded them to the truth of the heartfelt sentiment Daschle expressed. The marketplace needs more love. It is up to God's people to deliver it.

Endnotes

1. This account is adapted from "Civil War Split: Generals Made Hard Choices," by Charles F. Bryan, Jr., president, Virginia

Historical Society. Available at www. vahistorical.org/news/generals. htm. Used with permission.

2. From notes taken by coauthor Ken Walker at the "Lead Like Jesus" seminar at Southeast Christian Church, Louisville, Kentucky, Nov. 18, 2004.

3. Ibid.

4. Dennis Bakke, *Joy at Work* (Seattle, WA: Pearson Venture Group, 2005) 28.

CHAPTER 13

A Word for Pastors

*And He Himself gave some to be...pastors...for the equipping
of the saints* (Ephesians 4:11-12a).

A business executive from the Midwest—I'll call him Dwight—
came into the conference room where my seminar on Marketplace
Ministry was about to start. He looked like a kid on Christmas
morning.

"You'll never guess what happened!" he said, smiling. "I've
never seen anything like it. It was so awesome."

"What is it?" several people chimed in unison. "What happened?"

Turns out, the previous Sunday morning, Dwight's pastor
called a couple to the front of the church for prayer. Although this
is a regular occurrence, it generally involves someone who is leaving the country to become a missionary overseas, or a young student planning to enroll in seminary before going into the
pastorate.

"But this was different," Dwight said. "They weren't going anywhere; in fact, they weren't leaving their profession to join a church
staff. This was exactly the opposite. They're starting a new business,

and our pastor wanted to pray for them and ask the Lord to bless this ministry opportunity.

"This is the first time this has ever happened in our church," he continued, straining to contain his enthusiasm. "But I'm sure it won't be the last. All my business friends are riding high. Marketplace Ministry has made it into the Sunday morning service. They can hardly believe it. At last, a pastor has recognized that what they do is as valuable to God as what goes on inside a church building."

Grins spread across the faces of many in the audience. A few whistled or broke into spontaneous applause. Suddenly, Dwight broke into laughter and said, "Just kidding. But wouldn't it be wonderful if that were to happen?" Later, he confided to me, "That would never happen in our church. It's just a dream of mine."

Pastor, the question you need to ask yourself is: How many other business leaders embrace the same dream? Could the fictitious scene Dwight described unfold in your church? If not, you need to ponder what steps you can take to make it a reality. Something needs to happen to stem the tide of a legion of unhappy businesspersons departing from the traditional church. Many business leaders who know they are called by God to serve Him at work increasingly feel alienated from local congregations.

I offer my comments from a unique position at this stage of my life. I have served as a pastor for more than 40 years, the first 35 in a nuclear church setting. Now that I routinely visit 40 different congregations a year, I meet with dozens of pastors. And, through the seminars and conferences where I speak, I also have the opportunity to meet with numerous Christian business leaders.

This mixed audience provides me a broad perspective. Pastors in the traditional church perceive me as more of a Marketplace Minister than a pastor. Business leaders usually see me as a pastor, yet one who understands where they are coming from concerning the day-to-day business world. Because they trust me, members of both arenas feel free to candidly share their feelings about the church-business divide.

What I hear from pastors is the nearly unanimous lament that business leaders in their congregations are not that involved in ongoing ministry opportunities within the local church. Meanwhile, business leaders I talk to vent frustrations over not being understood or encouraged by their pastor in the ongoing ministry opportunities that exist in the workplace.

There is a crying need for more bridge building among both sides. Pastors feel threatened by the increasing "buzz" over ministry occurring outside the province of the local congregation. They harbor other fears, such as businesspersons' tithes going elsewhere or high-powered executives using the knowledge that they "are in ministry" to take over the church. Meanwhile, those in business are longing for practical training and encouragement as they pursue God's call in the marketplace.

No doubt there are control issues lurking in the background in both camps, as well as various insecurities. And so the gap continues to widen. As someone who cares deeply about both the nuclear and extended church, this breach affects me. There should not be two groups, only one Body of Christ with all its different facets, operating in harmony. Beyond that, pastors have much to offer business leaders, just as business leaders have much to offer pastors. The acrimonious relationship is crippling the Church at the very time it needs to take forward strides in reaching the world.

Thank goodness there are some exceptions to this scenario. I am fortunate to be a member of one of those churches who are reaching out to those in business. My pastor, Dick Bernal (of Jubilee Christian Center in San Jose, California) has released and trained business leaders for Marketplace Ministry. He also holds regular equipping sessions for those under his pastoral care. Recently when we spoke, he told me that he is writing a book to instruct other pastors in the care and shepherding of kings.

"Praise God," I replied. "We need it."

The Exodus

Unfortunately, outside the few exceptions utilizing businesspersons' gifts, the traditional, nuclear church is seeing a mass exodus. Rarely a week goes by that I don't meet, or hear about, another business leader who has "had it" and is leaving his or her congregation. The good news is they are not walking away from their faith in Christ, their determination to be involved in ministry, or even the Church at large. However, they no longer attend a local church and aren't searching for alternatives.

Pastors must grasp this fact: When someone says, "If you don't change, I will leave," it is not meant as a threat. Rather, it is both a warning and a plea. Businesspersons are asking that you educate yourself so that you can equip and train a powerful ministry tool that the Lord has placed within your grasp.

If you are asking yourself, "What steps can I take?" I hope my suggestions will be useful. When God first "downloaded" His word to me about the necessity of both kings (businesspeople) and priests (pastors) in carrying out His work in the ,marketplace, He also identified Marketplace Ministers who were touching their spheres of influence. When I started this journey in 1999, I knew next to nothing. I hope you will recognize that you are just as capable as me in learning and transforming your ideas and concepts about this field.

I see a three-step process in adopting a new outlook:

1. *Embrace a view for societal transformation.*

As a former pastor, I am intimately aware of the fact that pastors trained in traditional methods emphasize nuclear church growth instead of city and nationwide transformation. As long as your primary goal and ministry emphasis is on building your local congregation, you will never focus on training Marketplace Ministers. Step one in leaving the status quo behind is shifting your view from church growth to city transformation. What good is a thriving church if the society around it decays at an alarming rate?

2. *Educate and train yourself.*

I started by studying the Bible with a different mind-set, reading with a different set of lenses. When I started looking for marketplace messages, I found them everywhere. I was seeing things that I had not seen for the previous 35 years. Now they were there, on nearly every page and in every text.

For example, the story of the rich young ruler that appears in three of the Gospels is familiar to numerous church members. I had often preached on that passage and heard other pastors expound on it. To recap, the man asks Jesus how he can be assured of obtaining eternal life. After Christ lists a series of command-ments, the rich ruler essentially replies, "Been there, done that."

At that point, Jesus adds the clincher, "You still lack one thing. Sell all that you have and distribute to the poor, and you will have treasure in heaven; and come, follow Me" (Lk. 18:22). The com-mentary most preachers add goes like this: "It is clear that this man's money was keeping him out of Heaven. He needed to give it all away, but since it meant so much to him, he couldn't and went away full of sorrow." Once I heard a pastor say, "This man needed to leave the business that was keeping him away from God and go into the ministry."

The problem with such interpretations is they aren't consistent with the text. As you read this passage, notice that Jesus *did* tell the rich young ruler to sell all that he had. But He *did not* tell him to *give it all* to the poor. Think about it. If he sold everything and gave it all away, he would be poor, too. Next week someone else would need to sell everything so they could give to him.

What we have missed is the point of Christ's directive. The man was to sell everything and give some to the poor. What about the rest? He was to take care of his family, then invest in more products that he could sell, using those profits to again help the poor. His problem was not his love of money, but a lack of compassion.

This realization should motivate salespersons. Jesus wants you to sell all your products. When you make a profit, though, remem-ber to give to the poor. This encourages an ongoing business cycle:

- Invest in a product;

- Sell it for a profit so that you can invest in more product;

- As you do, take care of your family and those who are less fortunate.

In addition to taking a new perspective on Scripture, the growth of Marketplace Ministry has stimulated the writing of numerous books and other resources. I encourage you to pick up my first book *God@Work*; and then add *The God Factor* by Marcus Hester; *The Day of the Saints* by Bill Hamon; and *Anointed for Business* by Ed Silvoso. Sample some titles by powerful Marketplace Ministers, such as:

Frontline Christians in a Bottom-Line World by Linda Rios Brook.

Business Unlimited by Gunner Olsen.

Balancing Family, Faith and Work by Pat Gilsinger.

(A more complete listing appears in the Appendix.)

These materials will enhance your ability to pastor this new breed of Marketplace Minister. This will call for adjustments in your habits. Put aside some of your beloved theological texts and browse the lengthy list of Christian Marketplace books. Stretch yourself by reading a few business magazines and some popular business books. Further your education by staying in touch with the business community.

Also, sign up for some Marketplace conferences, both local and national. Because I speak several times a month at these meetings, I am well aware that in most cases pastors are conspicuously absent.

Often pastors will greet me, welcome me to the city, and then excuse themselves, saying they are much too busy that weekend to attend. They commonly add a comment like this: "But I know this isn't for me; this is for the marketplace folks. I have invited them and encouraged them to be here. Feel free to teach everything you want." Then they leave, blissfully unaware of the message they are sending to Marketplace Ministers.

Those in business quickly see that this conference is not a priority on the pastor's schedule, nor is it significant enough for the pastor to move into the #1 position. Yet, they also know how desperately the pastor needs to attend. They have been aching to hear a message about their impact in the workplace. They want to be effective and have come to this conference with high expectations. When the pastor leaves early, or doesn't even show up, it increases the divide between traditional church and marketplace.

3. *Understand that you cannot become a leader overnight to those who are far advanced in experience, practice, and knowledge.*

Years ago I heard a quote attributed to legendary Indian pacifist Mahatma Gandhi: "There go my people, and I must catch them, for I am their leader." This could be said of many pastors today. God has called you to lead—and you will—but there are some areas in which you must humble yourself. Become teachable.

There are areas where those you are called to equip have moved ahead, out of necessity. They now may be better equipped than you are. However, you don't have to remain that way. Prepare and educate yourself, asking your people such questions as:

- What do you want and need from me?
- What do I need to know in order to better equip you?
- What issues are you facing that I can address?

When I started teaching about the marketplace in the late 1990s, a large segment of our congregation quickly grabbed hold of the message. To them, this looked like manna from Heaven. Their excitement and anticipation greatly encouraged me. Any pastor can relate to the feeling I had, that I was hitting on all eight cylinders.

However, some of the most powerful business leaders in the congregation were the most resistant—not because they disagreed with the message, nor were they verbally or practically opposed. Yet they were obviously hesitant to jump on the bandwagon. These few influential people—the ones I had counted on to help move this train down the track—seemed the least interested. I expected them to be the leaders, but instead they were almost invisible. It took me awhile to grasp what was happening.

The Need for Equipping

I came to understand the reluctance of these businesspersons through a conversation with Linda Rios Brook. A former television executive, she teaches on Marketplace Ministry and has written several books about this field. The latest warns church leaders that they must quickly learn how to employ the talents of businesspersons in their congregations if they expect to keep them around.

Linda and I, along with spiritual leader C. Peter Wagner, pastor Chuck Pierce, and such business types as Os Hillman (director of the International Coalition of Workplace Ministries) and Kent Humphreys (president of the Fellowship of Companies for Christ International), had been speaking for a conference called Life-Works, a division of The Wagner Leadership Institute. Over a two-year period we had conducted half a dozen LifeWorks seminars, and while those who attended gave good evaluations, we were not attracting the crowds we expected.

Although we didn't realize it, the problem stemmed from our marketing approach. We were using the same kind of advertising Wagner and Pierce employed for their numerous conferences. That meant we were focusing on the nuclear church for our target audience, when we should have been going after the business world.

One afternoon Linda said, "You know, Rich, we have to change the way we advertise LifeWorks. We're asking pastors to invite their businesspeople to a conference. But when a business executive hears a pastor say, 'This is a great conference for the business leader,' he already knows the pastor doesn't have a clue about his life or ministry in business. So if the pastor thinks the conference is worthwhile, the businessperson says, 'I am not going.' "

Bingo! I suddenly realized why the most powerful Marketplace Ministers had not warmed to my messages. It wasn't because they disagreed with them. Rather, they had little confidence in my ability to bring them what they needed. Since they were better equipped than me, they were sitting back, watching and waiting. Subconsciously, they were saying to themselves, *I wonder how long this phase will last? How long will it be before he moves on to the next hot topic?*

Now that I have been studying, researching, and teaching on this subject for more than eight years, these same business leaders are rallying to the cause. They now want to know what is happening and are much more receptive to what I have to share with them. I now appreciate that before I could equip them, I needed to become prepared. I also needed to prove to them that I was in this for the long haul.

On a practical level, pastor, there are subtle ways to gain the confidence of Marketplace Ministers that is so necessary if you expect to lead them. Were I to become the pastor of a nuclear church again, here are some things I would do differently:

1. I would go to the workplace for appointments with businesspeople instead of always having these busy leaders come to my office. This would not only let them know how valuable they are, but it would enable me to see them in their everyday environment. It would allow me to pray with more insight and teach them on a more practical level.

2. I would make arrangements to pray at the various workplaces where my members serve. I wouldn't restrict these visits to a solo presence, either. I would ask intercessors and prophetic people to come with me and encourage them to seek God's guidance as they pray for these businesses' future impacts on the marketplace.

3. I would change the terminology that is common in the nuclear church.

4. I would teach on the key differences between the nuclear church and the extended church. I would shed the cliché of "full-time ministry" as applying solely to pastors, church staff members, and missionaries. Instead, I would emphasize that everyone is a full-time minister. Instead of calling it a "worship service" or "church service," I would call the weekly gathering an "equipping service." This would be more accurate and in line with the Lord's expectations. This new term would help emphasize that such gatherings are not the only form of worship or the sole expression of church.

5. During the weekly equipping service, I would institute a regular time of prayer for businesses. Depending on the size of the congregation and the city's makeup, I would either pray for a leading company or for several companies who employ members of the congregation. This would put a focus on ministry in the daily lives of the people. It would also send a message to the congregation and the city that we are concerned about their business.

Shepherding Horses

Training this special breed of minister will be unlike the normal work you are called to, and accustomed to, in your role as a pastor. Linda Rios Brook calls them "reds." Like the clothes in a laundry basket that will bleed all over the other colors, the "reds" may need to be separated for special treatment. This group is different and cannot be treated like everyone else. They are a very independent, self-confident, and energetic assembly. They will have opinions about everything. Based on those assumptions, they will act. Hesitate and they will run over you.

Kent Humphreys, who spent decades in business before joining FCCI, refers to the task of leading Marketplace Ministers as "shepherding horses." This is a much different process than shepherding "sheep"—the average church member/wage earner. Biblically, horses represent self-sufficiency (see Deut. 17:16) and fearlessness in battle (see Job 39:19-25). Horses also symbolize humans' best effort at obtaining what they want and need. Horses don't want to be shepherded and don't like to follow.

Yet, horses need training. And when they receive it, they can accomplish far more than sheep. It is these "reds" that pastors are called to lead. This challenging task requires building personal relationships of trust and understanding. Make them your friends and be a friend to them. Affirm their calling to the marketplace. Let them know that you respect them, are interested in their work, and are praying for them.

As with any paradigm shift, changes must take place in pastors' thinking, speaking, and actions:

1. *With regard to thinking, be open to adopting new mind-sets.*

Only by seeing issues in a new light can we make progress. For me, that meant evolving through several steps:

- moving from a philosophy of church growth to ministry in the marketplace,

- from simply ministering in the marketplace to having church in the marketplace,

- from church in the marketplace to ministry in all spheres of influence,

- from ministry in all spheres of influence to ministry to non-Christians in order to build relationships and make an impact for God's Kingdom.

Through this phase of thinking in a new way, God led me to develop model businesses that exemplify Kingdom practices. Thus, I received the idea to take biblically based and character-centered training into the marketplace. However, I saw the need to use non-religious terminology to develop these key relationships. (Imagine trying to do that in a traditional church setting.) As my outlook continues to shift towards Kingdom building, I realize that we can train leaders in the Christian community and the marketplace with the objective of transforming cities and nations.

2. *Our speaking must line up with our new thought processes.*

We must talk about transformation in every sphere of society. As we speak it, it will come to pass—that is, if we follow it up with action. Here are some things I encourage every pastor to do:

- Go to businesses for the purpose of prayer and learning.

- Listen and learn as you go. Marketplace Ministers have much to teach you.

- Humble yourself. Admit that you have not done a good job of equipping and assure your people you will improve.

- Repent and change.

- Begin a deliberate process for equipping your members to be ministers at work.

Because I know pastors so well, I recognize that some of you are ready to run out and start today. You are planning a sermon series on this topic and somehow believe you will complete this project in the next few weeks. Wrong! You are entering a lifestyle shift that demands a new style of ministry. This is not a quick fix. A few sermons, no matter how astute or inspiring, will not complete the task.

You cannot accomplish the equipping God wants you to do with preaching alone. As the apostle Paul told the church at Philippi, "The things which you have learned and received and heard and saw in me, these do…" (Phil. 4:9). The pattern Paul followed:

- First he taught the people.

- Then he made sure they received it—that they understood the heart of his message, not just sat and listened while letting his words pass in one ear and out the other.

- In addition, he wanted to make sure they had heard him—namely, that they not only heard what he said, but had internalized it and intended to act on his words.

- Paul also made sure they observed him in action. His teaching included demonstration, not just lecturing. He modeled a lifestyle, which needs to be part of the equipping process.

Setting an example is vital. A wise pastor will remember the lifestyle of Zadok, the priest King David called on to anoint his son as king. Zadok led a line of priests known for their holiness. In the forty-fourth chapter of Ezekiel, the prophet tells of a group of priests who strayed far from God and committed iniquity. Although the Lord would still allow them to continue in temple services, perform sacrifices, and stand before the people, their disobedience carried a high price.

As Ezekiel explains: "And they shall not come near Me to minister to Me as priest, nor come near any of My holy things, nor into the Most Holy Place; but they shall bear their shame and their abominations which they have committed" (Ezek. 44:13).

Later in the same chapter, Ezekiel reveals that only the sons of Zadok would stand before the Lord:

"But the priests, the Levites, the sons of Zadok, who kept charge of My sanctuary when the children of Israel went astray from Me, they shall come near Me to minister to Me; and they shall stand before Me to offer to Me the fat and the blood," says the Lord God. "They shall enter My sanctuary, and they shall come near My table to minister to Me, and they shall keep My charge. And it shall be, whenever they enter the gates of the inner court, that they shall put on linen garments; no wool shall come upon them while they minister within the gates of the inner court or within the house" (Ekekiel 44:15-17).

The number one trait required of those who would minister before the Lord is holiness. And the number one need in equipping Marketplace Ministers is to model a life of holiness. So, pastors, before you preach a sermon series or attempt to implement any plans of action—in fact, before you do anything—get on your knees before God and seek His direction. Ask Him to forgive you for failing to equip Marketplace Ministers. Commit to Him that you will follow a new way of ministry.

Pastors, I know that God can use you for great things. Just because earth-shattering change is coming to the Church does not mean He has forgotten the Church or is turning His back on you. I am confident that transformation will come to your city as you equip laypersons for ministry. The fear spreading through the world because of moral decay, terrorism, and fragmented families is simply another sign that the stage is set for the next Great Awakening. Get ready by joining God in the marketplace, where His work is exploding.

Appendix

Reading List

The Servant Leader by Ken Blanchard and Phil Hodges, published by J. Countryman.

Thank God It's Monday by Mark Greene, published by Scripture Union.

Thank God It's Monday by Rick Heeren, published by Transformational Publications (a division of Harvest Evangelism).

Releasing Kings for Ministry in the Marketplace by Harold Eberle and John Garfield, published by Worldcast Publishing.

On Kingdom Business by Tetsunao Yamamori and Ken Eldred, published by Crossway Books.

The Elk River Story, edited by Rick Heeren, published by Transformational Publications.

The Church Beyond the Congregation by James Thwaites, published by Paternoster Publishing.

Renegotiating the Church Contract by James Thwaites, published by Paternoster Publishing.

Church That Works by James Thwaites and David Oliver, published by Authentic Media.

Work: Prison or Place of Destiny by David Oliver, published by Authentic Media.

Changing Church by C. Peter Wagner, published by Regal Books.

Spheres of Authority by C. Peter Wagner, published by Wagner Publications.

Frontline Christians in a Bottom-Line World by Linda Rios Brook, published by Destiny Image.

Faith@Work by Os Hillman, published by Aslan Publishing.

God Is My CEO by Larry Julian, published by Adams Media Group.

Marketplace Ministers by Paul Gazelka, published by Creation House Press.

The God Factor by Marcus Hester, published by Destiny Image.

Lasting Investments by Kent Humphreys, published by NavPress Publishing.

Church on Sunday—Work on Monday by Laura Nash and Scotty McLennon, published by Jossey-Bass.

Christianity 9 to 5: Living Your Faith at Work by Michael Zigarelli, published by Beacon Hill Press.

Marketplace Christianity by Bob Fraser, published by _____.

Loving Monday: Succeeding in Business Without Selling Your Soul by John Beckett, published by InterVarsity Press.

Great Commission Companies by Steven L. Rundle, published by InterVarsity Press.

Business by the Book by Larry Burkett, published by Nelson Reference.

Doing Business God's Way by Dennis Peacock, published by Successful Christian Living.

True Wealth...By the Book by John Beehner, published by By the Book Publishing.

God's Ticker Tape by Ed Silvoso, published by Transformational Publications.

Anointed for Business by Ed Silvoso, published by Regal Books.

Business Unlimited by Gunner Olsen, published by International Christian Chamber of Commerce.

Balancing Family, Faith and Work by Pat Gelsinger, published by Life Journey.

How to Bring the Super to the Natural in the Marketplace by Dick Hochreiter, booklet available from www.faithandwork resources.com.

The Day of the Saints by Bishop Bill Hamon, published by Destiny Image.

Author Contact Information

Rich Marshall
441 Camille Circle, Suite 11
San Jose, CA 95134
Office: 408-230-3148
Cell: 408-432-8149
ROi
PO Box 640816
San Jose, CA 95164-0816
www.Godisworking.com
rich@Godisworking.com

Ken Walker
1355 Bardstown Rd., #217
Louisville, KY 40204
Email: Kenwalker33@cs.com
Fax: 502-585-1447
Cell: 502-930-1081

ALSO BY RICH MARSHALL

GOD@WORK: VOLUME ONE

God is showing up in places we have never imagined. We thought He was just for Sunday church or mid-week study. But God is showing up in small businesses and on construction sites, in schools and in politics. He is in factories and at checkout counters, at nurses' stations and the stock exchange. God is showing up everywhere outside of where we expect Him to be.

So what does it mean?

We serve a God who is not acting like we thought He should act.

This book is an awesome tool of discovery to learn not only what God wants, but how we can cooperate with His plan for the nations, not just the Church.

Discover how He wants you to step into a realm of ministry and fulfillment you have never dreamed possible. Learn how your work is the powerful dynamic of God's purposes for your life.

This book is the beginning of new possibilities for those who are willing to see that God is bigger than they thought He was.

ISBN 0-7684-2101-2

Additional copies of this book and other
book titles from DESTINY IMAGE are
available at your local bookstore.

For a complete list of our titles,
visit us at www.destinyimage.com
Send a request for a catalog to:

Destiny Image® Publishers, Inc.
P.O. Box 310
Shippensburg, PA 17257-0310

*"Speaking to the Purposes of God for This
Generation and for the Generations to Come"*